Cooking
Maine
Style

Down East Books

Published by Down East Books
An imprint of The Rowman & Littlefield Publishing Group, Inc.
4501 Forbes Blvd., Ste. 200
Lanham, MD 20706
www.rowman.com

Distributed by NATIONAL BOOK NETWORK

British Library Cataloguing in Publication Information available

Library of Congress Cataloging-in-Publication Data

Names: Oliver, Sandra L. (Sandra Louise), 1947- editor.
Title: Cooking Maine style : tried and true recipes from Down East / edited by Sandra Oliver.
Description: Camden, Maine : Down East, [2018]
Identifiers: LCCN 2018006703 (print) | LCCN 2018008831 (ebook) | ISBN 9781608939541 (e-book) | ISBN 9781608939534 (hardcover : alk. paper)
Subjects: LCSH: Cooking--Maine. | Cooking, American--New England style. | LCGFT: Cookbooks.
Classification: LCC TX715 (ebook) | LCC TX715 .C784219 2018 (print) | DDC 641.59741--dc23
LC record available at https://lccn.loc.gov/2018006703

™ The paper used in this publication meets the minimum requirements of American National Standard for Information Sciences—Permanence of Paper for Printed Library Materials, ANSI/NISO Z39.48-1992.

Printed in the United States of America

Cooking Maine Style

TRIED and TRUE RECIPES from DOWN EAST

MARJORIE STANDISH

Edited by Sandra Oliver

Down East Books

Camden, Maine

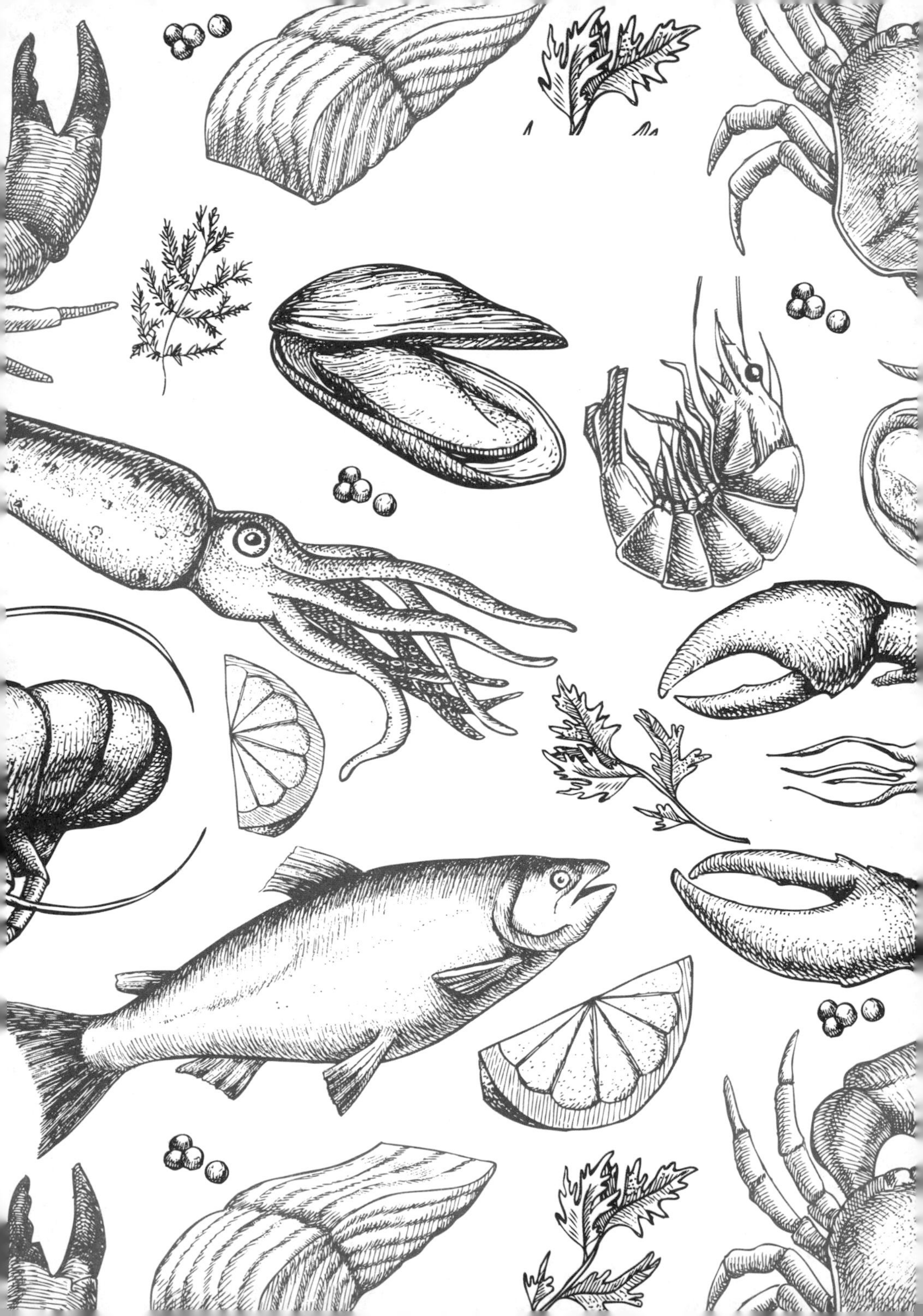

Contents

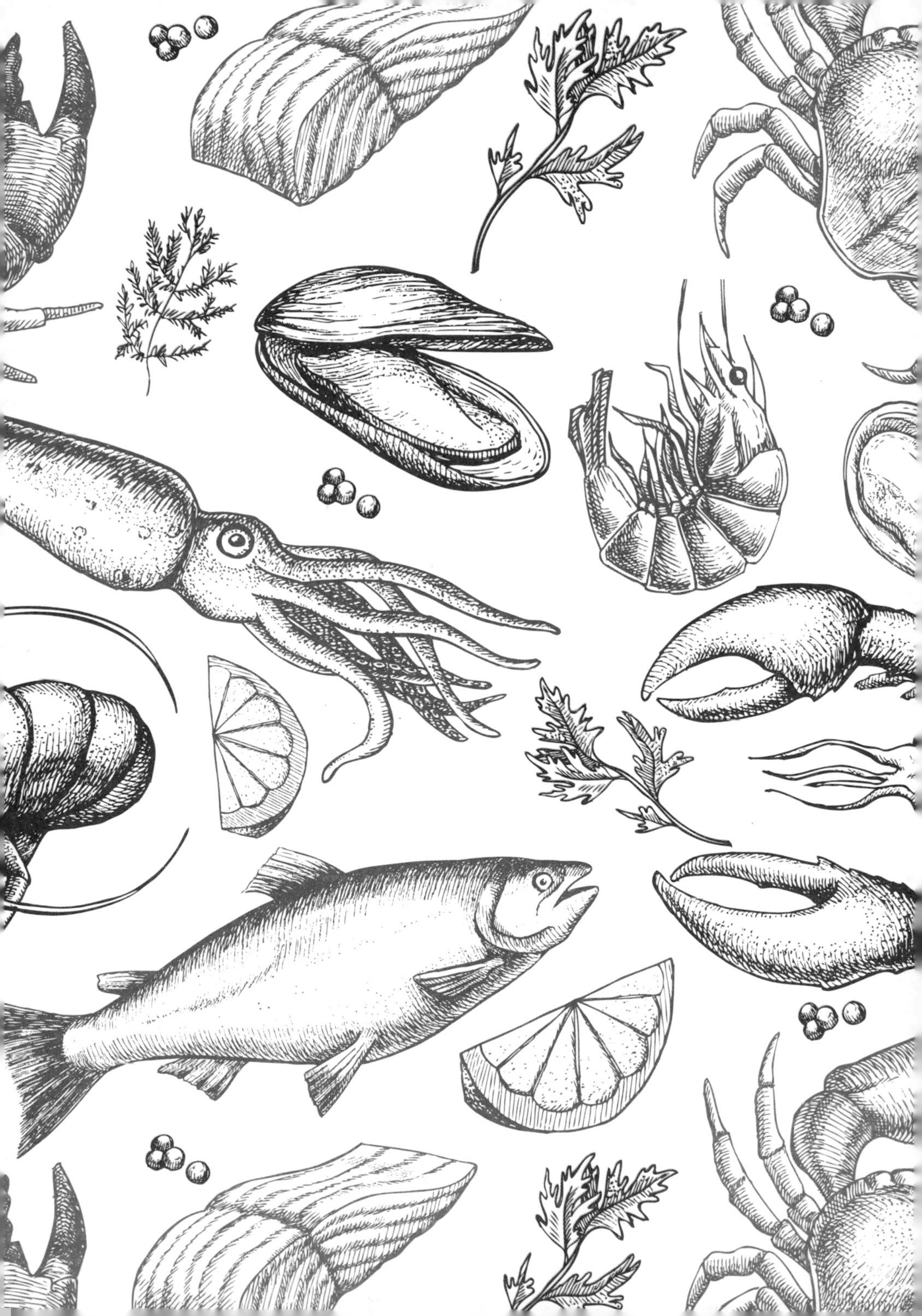

Foreword

Inside a tall fence in my backyard is a fairly expansive vegetable garden. There are fruit and nut trees, a hoop house for heat-loving vegetables, an area I call the "Back Forty" for growing potatoes and sprawling squashes, and two smaller beds named for my two favorite cookbook writers, Marjorie Standish and Helen Witty.

Helen Witty, besides having authored the most inspiring cookbooks on preserving and condiment making, mentored me through my first book writing venture some thirty years ago. Helen got me off to a good start in the business of food writing.

Marjorie Standish taught me about Maine cooking. Mrs. Standish is, or was, a fellow traveler in the weekly newspaper business with her *Maine Sunday Telegram* column, "Cooking Down East." And Mildred "Brownie" Schrumpf wrote a weekly cookery column for decades in the Bangor paper. I clump along in Brownie Schrumpf's *Bangor Daily News* footsteps with my column "Taste Buds." These two grand ladies, Marge and Brownie, each turned for recipes to their own memories, families, neighbors, and readers as I do, too. I also turn to them for inspiration and just plain good recipes worth keeping alive.

Mrs. Standish's *Cooking Down East*, a cookbook compiled from her column, appeared in 1969, twenty-one years after she began writing the column. Four years later, in 1973, she compiled a second cookbook, entitled *Keep Cooking the Maine Way*, which scooped up recipes her readers told her she should have put in the first book, or recipes she particularly liked and were significant to her column.

Her cookbooks have what we now call "legs," that is, a lasting quality. When in my own column, I query readers for a recipe for a particular Maine dish, often the recipes proffered can be traced back, sometimes word for word, to Mrs. Standish, although the sender may mention that "this recipe has been in my family a long time." No doubt it has.

An ever-dwindling number of Marge Standish's friends and colleagues are still alive.

Phillis Siebert, of Eastport, the Blaine House (Maine State Governor's mansion) chef from the 1970s to the 1990s, recalled Mrs. Standish visiting for tea. Ms. Siebert, who loved her job, remembered that Mrs. Standish would stop in the kitchen to chat. "She was a treasure for all those who cook and are learning to cook," Ms. Siebert wrote me. "I used many of her recipes over my twenty-seven years. We promoted Maine food products, so I incorporated them into her recipes as best I could. Blueberry gingerbread one of hers, was a favorite."

Another old friend, Pat Cunningham, who now lives in Orono, remembered that Marjorie and husband George were "our dear friends in our retirement years in Florida. Enjoyed her cooking and she mine."

Nancy Spooner of Amherst recalled that her dad George Winter was friends with George Standish, and that her mom clipped many of Mrs. Standish's Maine Sunday Telegram recipes out of the paper and stuck them into notebooks, a habit Nancy caught, too, she says.

Marjorie Standish grew up in Brunswick, Maine, and spent childhood summers at her family's old farm near the New Meadows River. She attended Farmington

State College, now the University of Maine at Farmington, studying Home Economics and graduating in 1931. She taught Home Ec. for a number of years in the western part of Maine, then worked for Central Maine Power as a "home service advisor," showing CMP customers show to use their new electric stoves. She and husband George lived in Gardiner for twenty-nine years before moving to Augusta just a couple years before *Cooking Down East* appeared. She picked up recipes everywhere she worked and lived: in Farmington when at school; Bridgeton, where she cooked at a summer camp; in Gardiner from many friends and neighbors; and from cooks all over the state who wrote to her; and from those who attended her cooking classes.

The twentieth century was a challenging time for cooks. Two world wars with their attendant rationing, and the Depression with its economically induced frugality put some food traditions on pause. Gee-whiz technical innovation followed in the 1950s and '60s, bringing processed convenience foods, frozen vegetables and home freezers, and cross-country transportation for seemingly unending supplies of fresh food year round. All these changes whisked cooks in Mrs. Standish's generation from cookery on wood-fueled cook stoves to electric and gas ranges; from summers spent in vegetable gardens, home-canning produce, and storing vegetables in cellars for the winter to supermarkets full year-round with California and Florida-grown vegetables and fruit.

While Mrs. Standish wrote about her girlhood and happily recalled the smell of beans baking in the old cook stove, brown bread bubbling in a kettle, and red flannel hash frying in an iron skillet, she lived in a time of casseroles and canned soups that made handy sauces in a hurry. She and her peers made good use of them, as did my mother. With the spare time not spent in the kitchen, women in her generation pursued careers, sustained volunteer organizations, enjoyed companionate marriages and leisure activities. Mrs. Standish, in addition to work as a cooking teacher and writer, was an avid golfer.

Still, in her writing, we can detect tension between the "from scratch" cookery she grew up with and respected, and what she called "now" cookery, employing prepared foods and modern ingredients. She often comments on this in recipe notes. And when we read lists of ingredients calling for margarine or vegetable shortening, which today have a less desirable reputation, we might dismiss her recipes as hopelessly out of date. That would be a pity, because food has fashions as surely as clothing, furnishings, and language do, and we can get a glimpse of a time past that some of us may remember from our childhoods, and from which younger ones may gain an understanding of a time now rejected.

Like Mrs. Standish, I love the old fashioned, classic Maine dishes like chowders, baked beans, and hermits. In selecting recipes for this volume, I tended to favor them because the food historian in me hopes to preserve worthwhile traditional recipes. Plenty of the recipes she wrote have terrific utility for today's cooks and I included many of them. In each chapter that follows are recipes I think of as typical of the 1950s and 60's, and I chose some of them as examples of an era, and labeled them "A Period Piece." Read and enjoy, or give them a try for a taste of vintage cooking.

This volume is organized exactly as Mrs. Standish organized her cookbooks, with extracts from each chapter under the same chapter titles Mrs. Standish used. Besides selecting recipes for their intrinsic historical value, I also chose recipes that she indicated were key recipes in her newspaper career or particularly memorable to her personally. Recipes with Maine place names interested me, too, and I added several of those.

Please read and enjoy. Cook and taste, too. We all can use a few ideas for what to make for our own suppers, and we'll want to keep cooking the Maine way, too.

Sandra Oliver
Islesboro, Maine

1 Stews, Chowders, and Soups

It wouldn't be cooking [Maine style] if this first chapter were anything but stews, chowders, and soups. . . . In many years of writing the newspaper column "Cooking Down East," I have learned these are the recipes you want to use in your own homes.

MAINE LOBSTER STEW

Boil 2 one-pound Maine lobsters and remove meat immediately, saving also the tomally (or liver), the coral, and the thick white substance from inside the shell.

Using a heavy kettle, simmer the tomally and coral in ½ cup butter for about 8 minutes. Then add lobster meat cut in fairly large pieces.

Cook all together slowly, using a low heat for about 10 minutes.

Remove from the heat or push to back of stove and cool slightly. Then add very slowly, 1 quart rich milk, stirring constantly.

Allow the stew to stand, refrigerated 5 or 6 hours before reheating for serving. This is one of the secrets of truly fine flavor. It's called aging.

Serves 4.

SHRIMP STEW

Substituting our Maine shrimp for the lobster in a stew is a fine way of preparing this delicacy. Because we like to serve these shrimp at their best, it is wise to use raw shrimp in making a stew for the best flavor. Maine shrimp do not need to be deveined.

Use peeled raw Maine shrimp, cook in butter just as you would in making any Maine stew. Do this slowly, the shrimp are cooked when they lose their glassiness and curl up. This takes about 2 or 3 minutes.

Add milk slowly. Heat to boiling point, add salt and pepper to taste.

Serves 4.

QUAHOG STEW

A quahog is a hard-shelled round clam. Large quahogs are known as "chowders," medium-sized quahogs are called "cherrystones," and small quahogs are "littlenecks."

1 quart milk, or 3 cups milk and one cup light cream

½ cup butter

1 pint shucked quahogs with liquor (cooking sherry)

¼ teaspoon black pepper

½ teaspoon salt

Scald the milk. While it is heating, melt the butter in a saucepan. Cut up the quahogs by placing them on a small wooden board and with a paring knife cut each one into several small pieces.

Add the raw quahogs, which have been chopped fine and the liquor to the melted butter. Simmer the butter, quahogs, and liquor together about 3 minutes.

Add to heated milk. Add salt and pepper. Taste, to be sure of seasoning. Serve at once with crackers.

Serves 4.

OYSTER STEW

1 pint oysters

6 tablespoons butter

1 tablespoon Worcestershire sauce

½ teaspoon celery salt

1½ pints to 1 quart milk

Salt to season, after the stew is made

½ to 1 teaspoon paprika

Put raw oysters in saucepan. Add butter and seasonings. Stir and bring quickly to a boil, lower heat, continue stirring and cooking, not longer than 2 minutes, allowing the edges of the oysters to curl.

Add milk, bring again to just below boiling point, but do not allow to boil (or it could curdle).

Dip into bowls, add another pat of butter to each bowl if you wish, sprinkle with paprika. Serve with oyster crackers.

Serves 2 amply. If you use a quart of milk it will serve 4 skimpily.

MAINE CLAM CHOWDER

The old recipes always advised us to allow chowder to ripen in refrigerator several hours or a day. Then reheat it slowly over a very low heat. But now that we use homogenized milk the ripening period often is omitted to avoid danger of the chowder separating, a problem sometimes associated with use of homogenized milk. The use of evaporated milk as given in some recipes also helps to avoid curdling.

MAINE CLAM CHOWDER

- 1 quart fresh Maine clams, shucked raw
- 2 thin slices salt pork
- 1 small onion, diced in small pieces
- 4 cups diced (small) potatoes
- 1 cup water or enough to just show up through the potatoes
- Salt and pepper
- 1½ quarts milk
- 1 tall can evaporated milk
- Piece of butter
- Common crackers

Using a kettle, fry out salt pork on a low heat. Remove pork and cook diced onion slowly in fat, taking care not to burn it. Add the four cups diced potatoes and the water, better add a little salt and pepper right now. Cover kettle, bring to steaming point, lower heat, cook until potatoes are soft; about 15 minutes.

In the meantime, using cutting board and a sharp knife, cut the head of each clam in two or three pieces. Do the same with the firm part of the clam and the soft part or belly also—No, I do not remove the black part. Save any juice you can.

When potatoes are soft, stir in the cut clams. Add 1 ½ quarts of milk and the evaporated milk. Taste for seasoning, add salt and pepper if necessary. Keep in mind that as the chowder ripens it may be salty enough. Add piece of butter or margarine.

Serve chowder with common crackers, pilot crackers, or Maine blueberry muffins.

Serves 6.

FISH CHOWDER WITH OLD FASHIONED FLAVOR

Good old Maine custom dictates that reheated pork bits be scattered on top of chowder. But you may serve them in a separate dish in case someone votes against the idea.

¼ pound salt pork, diced

2 onions sliced or diced

4 cups potatoes,
in small pieces

1 or 2 cups water

2 pounds fish fillets
(haddock, cod, or cusk)

1 teaspoon salt

¼ teaspoon pepper

¼ teaspoon Accent

2 or 3 cups whole milk

1 tall can evaporated milk

Fry diced salt pork slowly in bottom of heavy kettle until golden colored. Remove pork scraps and set aside. There should be about 3 tablespoons fat in the kettle.

Add onions and cook until yellowed (but not brown). Add potatoes and enough water so it comes nearly to top of potatoes. Place fish on top of potatoes, sprinkle with seasonings. Cover, bring to a boil, then cook on low heat until potatoes are tender and fish "flakes."

Pour in both kinds of milk and allow to heat thoroughly, but not boil.

Serves 6.

SALMON CHOWDER (A PERIOD PIECE)

We say, "try out" salt pork. It means to cook slowly, using a low heat.

2 slices salt pork

3 or 4 slices onion diced

3 cups diced potatoes

Salt and pepper

1 cup water

1 tall can salmon

1 quart milk

Lump of butter (approx. 2 tablespoons)

Cook slices of pork until fat is "tried out." Cook onion until golden in fat after removing pork slices (If you prefer, a half stick of margarine may be used as the fat for cooking onion in place of the salt pork). Add water to kettle, add raw potato, salt and pepper. Cover kettle and bring to steaming point. Cook on low heat about 15 minutes or until potato is tender.

Use pink, medium, or red salmon. The buying public has come to think of red salmon as the only first class salmon, but this is not the case. Pink salmon used in this chowder is delicious and a lot less expensive.

Break up canned salmon, removing skin and bones. Leave salmon in as large chunks as possible. Add salmon to kettle. Stir lightly, add milk. Add piece of butter or margarine. Taste for seasoning.

The longer this chowder ages, the better. You will like its pink color. Serve with common crackers if available.

POTPOURRI SOUP (A PERIOD PIECE)

This is one of the most popular soups I have ever used in my column. Hearty and delicious, it is made with hamburg. Or, if you just happen to have any—venison.

3 tablespoons butter or margarine

¾ pound hamburg or venison-burger

3 onions, sliced

⅓ cup barley

1 No. 2 can tomatoes

1½ quarts water

1 tablespoon salt

½ teaspoon black pepper

A few whole peppercorns, if you have them

3 carrots sliced

3 potatoes, diced

3 stalks celery, diced

1 teaspoon steak sauce

1 teaspoon Worcestershire sauce

Using a large soup kettle, fry meat in melted fat until the red color leaves it, crumbling meanwhile so that meat is separated.

Add onions and cook for a few minutes longer. Add water, tomatoes, barley, salt, and pepper. Cover and simmer gently over a low heat for 1 hour.

Add vegetables, Worcestershire, and steak sauces, bring back to steaming point, lower heat and cook for another hour. Serve hot with corn bread or biscuits.

Makes 6 servings of ample proportions.

OLD-FASHIONED SPLIT PEA SOUP

Pea soup was always served with johnnycake and still is. After all, when you combine the economy of this rich, wholesome soup with the solid comfort of johnnycake, you've got a real meal going.

1 pound dried split peas, yellow or green

1 onion

1 carrot

1 potato

Salt

Pepper

2 quarts water

Wash peas and put in kettle; cut and add vegetables. Add seasonings and water. If ham stock is available, use that and 3 tablespoons fat; otherwise use a ham bone or smoked pork chop or ¼ pound salt pork.

Cover kettle, bring to steaming point, lower heat, and cook slowly for 3 to 4 hours. Stir occasionally, to prevent scorching.

Remove meat and fat. Strain soup, pressing vegetables through sieve, or use a food mill. Cut any bits of ham or smoked pork chop, if used, and add to soup. Add 1 cup cold milk and reheat.

Serves 6.

SPIDER JOHNNYCAKE

¾ cup cornmeal

¼ cup sifted flour

1 tablespoon sugar

½ teaspoon salt

1 teaspoon baking powder

1½ cups, plus 2 tablespoons milk

1 egg, well beaten

2 tablespoons margarine

Sift dry ingredients. Add 1 cup plus 2 tablespoons milk and beaten egg, Mix only enough to dampen dry ingredients.

Melt margarine in frypan or 8 x 8-inch pan. Turn mixture into pan, pour remaining ½ cup milk over batter. Do not stir.

Bake at 400 degrees for 25 to 30 minutes. Serve piping hot.

Serves 4.

TOMATO BISQUE

- 2 cups canned tomatoes
- 4 cups milk
- 4 tablespoons butter or margarine
- Pepper
- Salt
- 1 teaspoon sugar

Put tomatoes in saucepan, juice too, chop tomatoes into small pieces. Add the butter, sugar, pepper and salt, bring to a boil.

Boil about 5 minutes. Add milk and bring again to a boil. Serve as is, without straining. Don't ask me why it doesn't curdle, but it doesn't.

Serves 6.

PARSNIP STEW

I like [parsnips] best when a neighbor or friend lets them stay in his garden all winter, then digs them to share as a very special part of springtime in Maine.

2 slices salt pork (or use 2 tablespoons margarine or butter)

1 small onion, diced

2 cups diced potatoes

2 cups water

Salt and pepper to taste

3 cups parsnip, cut in cubes

1 quart milk

4 tablespoons margarine

Try out salt pork over low heat. Remove pieces of pork, add onion, and cook gently. Add diced potatoes, water, salt, and pepper; cover kettle, bring to steaming point.

Cook potatoes 10 minutes, then add cubed parsnips, which do not take long to cook. Return cover and cook for 10 minutes after steaming point is again reached.

Test for doneness and add milk. Season to taste. Add margarine or butter, if it has not been used in place of salt pork. Some cooks like to add ½ cup rolled-out cracker crumbs for thickening.

Serve topped with minced parsley.

Serves 6.

SEAFOOD CHOWDER

The top of a double boiler is excellent for keeping chowders until serving time and leaves far less chance of curdling or "separation." This holds for any stew or chowder where milk is involved.

2 slices salt pork

1 small onion, diced

2 cups water or bottled clam juice

3 cups pared and diced potatoes

1 pound haddock fillets

Salt and pepper

½ pound scallops

1 pint chopped clams, or 2 cans minced clams

1 can crabmeat or

2 cups fresh lobster meat or

2 cups Maine shrimp

2 quarts milk, scalded

1 stick butter or margarine

Try out salt pork in kettle, remove pork scraps, and cook diced onion in fat, gently. Add water or clam juice and potatoes, cover and cook about 15 minutes.

Lay haddock fillets and fresh scallops on top of potatoes, simmer slowly just until fish flakes and scallops are done. It is best to quarter the scallops before placing them in the kettle. If clams are uncooked, then they go into kettle at the same time. If canned clams are used, then they are added with crabmeat, cooked lobster meat, or cooked shrimp.

Add scalded milk, stick of butter or margarine. Taste for seasoning.

Serves 8 to 10.

2 Fish and Shellfish

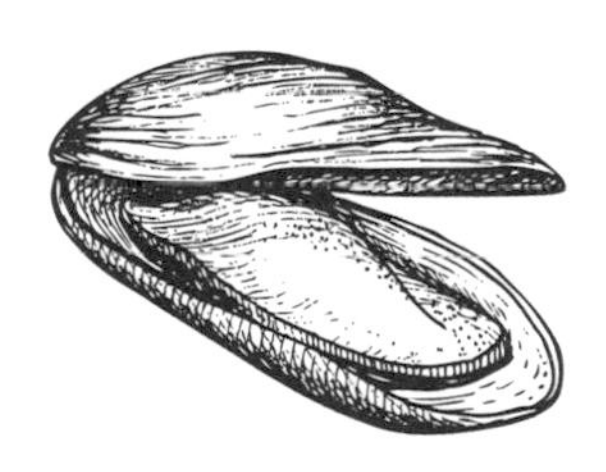

When Marjorie Standish was a child, her family went motor-boating on the New Meadows River near Brunswick. She wrote, "Dad knew every bit of the New Meadows and he liked to tell us who owned cottages and other points of interest. We liked to buy lobsters at Ed Holbrook's store at Cundy's Harbor. Sometimes we bought fish, if we had not done any fishing ourselves."

She observed that the family outings on the New Meadows River were more fun than almost anything else her family did together and that, "Maine seafood and fish recipes take on an added interest when they have been part of your life since childhood."

ROLLED HADDOCK FILLETS

6 haddock fillets

Butter or margarine

1½ cups soft bread crumbs

2 tablespoons minced onions

2 tablespoons minced parsley

Salt and pepper

Hot water to moisten dressing.

Salt haddock fillets, spread with dressing; roll up and secure with toothpicks.

Bake at 450 degrees for 30 minutes. Serve with egg sauce (see below).

Serves 4 to 6.

4 tablespoons butter

4 tablespoons flour

½ teaspoon salt

Dash of pepper

2 cups milk

2 hard-cooked eggs

EGG SAUCE

Melt butter, add flour, seasonings and blend well. Add milk slowly, stirring constantly.

Cook over low heat until thickened. Cut hard-cooked eggs in small pieces and add.

FISH SPENCER

6 fish sticks (choose nice fat ones)

1 egg

2 tablespoons milk

Salt and pepper

Butter or margarine

Cornflakes, rolled

Wipe fish sticks, season, dip in egg which has been slightly beaten and combined with milk; roll in cornflakes.

Lace in well-buttered baking dish, dot generously with butter or margarine.

Bake about 30 minutes at 450 degrees.

Serves 3 to 4.

SALMON LOAF

Back when I was going cooking schools this was one of my favorite recipes. Or you could make salmon wiggle.

1 large can red salmon

½ teaspoon salt

¼ teaspoon paprika

¼ teaspoon pepper

3 tablespoons lemon juice

3 egg whites

¼ cup melted butter or margarine

3 egg yolks

1½ cups firmly packed soft bread crumbs

1½ cups scalded milk

Remove skins and bones from salmon and mash very fine. Mix salmon, paprika, pepper, salt, lemon juice, melted butter, beaten egg yolks, and bread crumbs. Add hot milk, fold in stiffly beaten egg whites.

Pour into greased loaf pan. Bake at 375 degrees for 1 hour. Serve with egg sauce.

Serves 8.

SALMON WIGGLE

- 4 tablespoons margarine or butter
- 4 tablespoons flour
- ¼ teaspoon pepper
- ½ teaspoon salt
- 2 cups milk
- 1 can red salmon
- 1 can peas, drained, or
- 1 package frozen peas, cook

Prepare cream sauce by melting margarine or butter, adding flour, salt, and pepper. Stir until smooth. Add 2 cups milk, gradually. Cook over low heat, stirring constantly, until smooth and thickened.

Add drained peas. Add salmon that has been picked over, bones and skin removed. Keep salmon in fairly large pieces. Serve on buttered toast, toast cups, patty shells, crackers, or baked potatoes.

Serves 4 to 6.

FISH CAKES

Ever wonder what Maine mothers and grandmothers served with baked beans on Saturday night before the days of the hot dog? Many of course felt baked beans, brown bread, pickles with cake for dessert was ample. Yet if men worked hard all day on Saturday as they did not too many years ago, most housewives felt baked beans needed an additional dish to make Saturday night supper more hearty. Codfish cakes filled this need. . . . I remember fish cakes best when my mother had prepared them and placed them on a platter ready to be fried to a golden brown. They looked all "Whiskery."

1 box or 1 pound salt codfish

4 or 5 medium sized potatoes

¼ teaspoon pepper

1 egg

Soak salt codfish overnight in water to cover. In morning, drain dish, add peeled potatoes, sliced about ½ inch thick. Add about 1 cup cold water, bring to a boil together and cook until potatoes are done. About 15 minutes.

Drain in a colander and return to saucepan. Mash fish and potatoes together, add whole egg and pepper and beat with a silver fork. With a tablespoon scoop up the mixture and shape with the silver fork so that the cakes are "whiskery." Slide onto a platter. Place in a cool spot until ready to fry.

To fry, melt ¼ inch of shortening in skillet. Fry until crusty gold on each side, turning once.

Serves 6.

SALT COD DINNER

Probably no old-style Maine dinner brings more favorable comments than a salt codfish dinner. The salt codfish is placed on a platter with pork scraps, surrounded with boiled potatoes of uniform size and small buttered or sliced beets, the fish topped with a plain or egg sauce, not only looks good, it is good.

1 pound salt cod

6 medium-sized Maine potatoes

6 medium-sized beets

4 tablespoons all-purpose flour

¼ pound salt pork

2 cups milk

¼ teaspoon pepper

Soak salt codfish overnight to freshen it. If time is a factor, then place dried salt codfish in a kettle, add about 1 quart cold water. Heat this to just about the boiling point, but do not boil. Pour off this water and do it all over again. You probably will want to do this a third time, too. Taste fish to be certain it is not too salty.

After freshening fish by either method, simmer it just below the boiling point until fish is tender. This will take only a few minutes. Remember this fish should never be boiled, it makes it tough. The fish is done if it flakes when broken.

Boil the potatoes. Boil and dice or slice the beets, or use canned beets.

SALT COD DINNER

Wash the ¼ pound salt pork, then dice. Cook salt pork very slowly in a frying pan over low heat. Drain the pork and return about 4 tablespoons of the fat to frying pan.

Add 4 tablespoons flour to the fat and stir. Add pepper. Add milk slowly, stirring constantly so that the gravy will be smooth. Add a little salt if necessary. Keep this gravy hot. At this point, the cooked salt cod may be added to this gravy or served in the following manner.

TO SERVE SALT COD

Placed freshened, cooked fish on a hot platter. Place the crispy bits of fried salt pork on top of the fish. Make a red border of beets around the fish. Serve the gravy and cooked potatoes separately, or, if you prefer, the gravy may be poured over the fish, then the crispy salt pork sprinkled on top of this.

Better serve johnnycake with this, hadn't you?

Serves 6.

FINNAN HADDIE CASSEROLE [A PERIOD PIECE]

3 pounds finnan haddie (smoked fillets) soaked in cold milk to cover

3 cups cooked rice

2 cans Welsh rarebit or
2 cans cheese soup or
2 packages frozen Welsh rarebit

2 cups of milk (to mix with rarebit)

Grated cheese

Buttered crumbs

Place smoked fillets in a large saucepan. Cover with cold milk and soak for 1 hour. Place pan on heat and simmer until fish flakes. Spoon milk over fish occasionally as it heats. Discard this milk, as it's too salty to use.

Cook enough dry rice so that you will have 3 cups of cooked rice. Mix the 2 cups of milk with Welsh rarebit and combine with 3 cups cooked rice.

With a slotted spoon lift the smoked fish, keeping it in as large flakes as possible and place in a large buttered casserole. Lightly mix with the cooked rice and cheese mixture. Grate American cheese over top. Top with buttered crumbs.

Bake at 350 degrees for 30 minutes. I think of this as adult fare.

Serves 8, generously.

SCALLOPED OYSTERS

1 pint oysters

1¼ cups rolled crackers

½ cup melted margarine or butter

1 cup milk

Salt and pepper

Clean oysters thoroughly. Cook in own liquor over low heat until edges curl. Remove oysters to a bowl, leaving liquor in saucepan. Add 1 cup milk to liquor. Let come to boiling point, then add margarine or butter.

Meanwhile, chop oysters or cut each oyster into 3 or 4 pieces. Roll in cracker crumbs. Reserve ¼ cup of the crumbs to mix with melted margarine for topping.

Using a shallow baking pan, place a layer of crumbs. Then oysters in the pan. Sprinkle with salt and pepper. Repeat with another layer of crumbs, oysters, and seasonings. Pour heated milk and melted margarine or butter over all.

Top with buttered crumbs. Bake at 400 degrees for 30 minutes.

Serves 4.

SARDINE STUFFED TOMATO CUPS

"A tin of Maine sardines is a good traveling companion and they are good for you," wrote Mrs. Standish, who also provided two recipes for preparing them-one for Tossed Sardine Salad and the following one for Stuffed Tomato Cup. At the time she published Cooking Down East there were still many sardine packing plants in coastal Maine towns and Maine sardines were widely available. Today, no sardine packing plants are left though sardines are available in stores, and they are still "good for you."

2 tins, Maine sardines

⅓ cup diced celery

1 tablespoon diced onion

2 tablespoons salad dressing

4 drops Tobasco sauce

½ teaspoon Accent

4 small tomatoes

Open the tins of Maine sardines, reserve 4 whole sardines. Drain. Add celery, onions, salad dressing, Tobasco sauce and Accent. Mix well.

Peel tomatoes and scoop out small section, fill cavity with sardine mixture. Top with whole sardine.

Makes 4 Tomato Cups.

STEAMED CLAMS

I never saw anyone who enjoyed digging clams, getting them ready for steaming, serving, and eating them any more than my Dad. . . . He liked doing it himself, too. Didn't want women folks bothering around at all. He knew at just what point the oval, thin-shelled Maine clams were ready. He relied on no one else's judgement. Neither did we!

Scrub clams with a stiff brush. Be sure they are rinsed carefully to get rid of that last bit of mud or sand. Do each clam separately is a good rule for delicious steamed clams.

Place clams in a large kettle and add cold water, but only enough to cover the bottom of the kettle. Otherwise how do you expect to get true clam water? The general rule is ½ cup cold water to each 4 quarts of clams in the shell. Cover tightly. Bring to steaming point.

Cook over low heat for 10 to 20 minutes until shells open. To test for doneness? No better way than eating one, hot as it is! Serve with melted butter—and clam water.

CLAM CAKES

1 pint chopped clams

1½ cups cracker crumbs

2 eggs unbeaten

Mix clams and crumbs together. Add eggs one at a time and mix well. Let stand for a few minutes to soften crumbs. Mixture should hold together and be moist.

Fry in butter in a frypan. Drop in large spoonfuls of the mixture, press down with a spoon to make cakes ¾ inch thick. Fry on one side until brown, turn and brown other side. If common crackers are used, season with salt. Do not add salt if saltines are used. The liquid from the clams may be used and adds flavor.

Serves 4.

SIMPLY BAKED SCALLOPS

Wash scallops, wipe dry, and place in a shallow baking dish. Salt and pepper scallops. Pour milk into pan to the depth of about ½-inch.

Bake at 400 degrees for 20 minutes. Serve with baked potatoes, scalloped tomatoes, celery for an easy supper or dinner.

Serves 4.

BOOTHBAY HARBOR CRAB CAKES

In spite of the popularity of fresh crabmeat salad rolls, or, for that matter, of fresh crabmeat salad, probably there is no more popular use of fresh Maine crab than this crab cake recipe that was chosen to appear in the first *State of Maine Best Seafood Recipes*. These crabmeat cakes could hardly miss, especially when served with lobster sauce.

1½ cups crab meat

3 eggs separated

1 cup cracker crumbs or soft bread crumbs

½ teaspoon salt

Dash of pepper

¼ cup melted butter

2 teaspoons lemon juice

1 teaspoon minced green pepper

1 teaspoon minced celery

Mix crabmeat, beaten egg yolks, crumbs, melted fat, and all seasonings. Blend thoroughly. Fold in stiffly beaten egg whites.

Turn mixture into 4 well-greased custard cups. Set them in a pan of hot water and bake at 375 degrees for 25 minutes. Unmold and serve with lobster sauce.

LOBSTER SAUCE

To 1 cup hot medium white sauce add ½ cup finely cut cooked lobster. Heat well and pour over hot crab cakes.

Serves 4.

STATE OF MAINE BOILED LOBSTER

Have 2 inches boiling water in a large kettle. Add 1 to 2 tablespoons salt, depending upon number of lobsters and size of kettle. Plunge live and kicking lobsters in, hold downward. Cover kettle, bring quickly back to steaming point. Time 16 to 18 minutes for 1-pound size and 18 to 20 minutes for 1¼- to 1½-pound lobsters.

Remove from water and place each lobster on its back to drain. Serve hot with melted butter. If you serve them cold, use mayonnaise in place of melted butter.

LOBSTER CASSEROLE

I remember when my Farmington roommate used this recipe for Maine lobster casserole for the very first time. She served it to the directors of the Central Maine Power Company for a luncheon at the annual meeting a long, long time ago. Since then the popularity of the casserole has grown and grown. After all, when you have a group of men telling about the goodness of a casserole, you can be certain it is.

3 tablespoons butter

1 pound cooked lobster meat.

3 tablespoons flour

¾ teaspoon dry mustard

3 slices white bread, crust removed

2 cups rich milk, part cream

Salt and pepper to taste

Cut lobster in bite size pieces and cook slowly in butter to start pink color. Do not cook too long or too fast or it will toughen. Remove lobster meat.

Add flour mixed with seasonings to fat in pan. Add rich milk slowly. Cook stirring constantly until thickened. Add lobster and bread torn into pieces.

Turn into buttered casserole. Top with a few buttered crumbs and bake at 350 degrees for about 30 minutes or until bubbly and delicately browned. If desired, a tablespoon or two of sherry may be added to the mixture.

Serves 4.

3 Poultry

"In thinking back over the twenty years that I have been writing 'Cooking Down East,' I expect the greatest change in Maine's food picture has been with chicken," wrote Mrs. Standish in her first cookbook. She noted that chicken eating was a luxury because most chickens were grown to become hens for eggs, and when a hen "outlived her usefulness," the cook might make fricassee, chicken pie, pressed chicken, or salad. "Then came the change and we became a chicken producing state. We produce a tender, plump, meaty, and delicately flavored bird for your eating pleasure. Maine chicken is a quality food product grown for meat purposes only, now obtainable year-round, fresh or quick frozen and government inspected."

In midcoast Maine, where I live, the countryside is still dotted with the remains of the chicken-raising houses that abounded in the 1950s and '60s. Belfast's chicken plants employed many people until the industry moved south to Maryland and then farther into the deep South, where it thrives today. Friends my age tell of times when chicken trucks rolled down the roads of Waldo County with feathers fluttering out behind, and the Passagassawaukeg River was red with blood from chicken processing.

Plentiful and cheap chicken—especially boneless, skinless breasts—is terribly popular today, easy to prepare, and susceptible to lots of recipe variations. I doubt Mrs. Standish would be surprised.

OLD FASHIONED CHICKEN PIE

Use about six pounds of chicken. Prepare chicken for cooking and simmer in about one quart of water with salt and pepper added.

Cook until chicken practically falls off bone. When cool enough, remove meat from bones, leaving in rather large pieces. You may then store in covered pan for a day or make the chicken pie right away. If you prepare chicken the day before, then cool broth and store separately.

Thicken the broth as follows: Mix six tablespoons flour with cold broth, add a small amount of broth at a time. Cook over low heat, stirring constantly until thickened.

Make a regular pie crust (or use a mix if you wish). Line bottom and sides of a large casserole with pastry. Do not roll crust too thin. Place pieces of chicken in crust. Pour thickened gravy all over the chicken. Lay pastry on top. Flute edges together. Be sure to cut several vents in the top crust.

Bake at 425 degrees for 40 minutes. Serve piping hot!

Serves 8 to 10.

BEAN POT CHICKEN BREASTS

1 stick butter or margarine

4 or 5 chicken breasts, halved

Salt, pepper, and poultry seasoning

1 onion, peeled

Using your bean pot or a heavy covered casserole, place the stick of margarine in bottom of it. Place the whole peeled onion in next.

Prepare chicken breast for cooking. (If you take advantage of the chicken sales, then you probably have bought breasts with wings attached. Remove tips of wings and disjoint wings from breast halves and cook separately in bean pot. The breasts look better when served and fit into the bean pot more easily without the wings. Leave skin on breasts and wings.)

Salt and pepper chicken, sprinkle with poultry seasoning. Lay bone side up on top of margarine and onion. No browning, no water. Cover bean pot or casserole. Place in 300-degree oven and bake for about 4 hours. You could even use 275 degrees and a 5-hour period. Isn't this great?

If you wish, serve rice and cook it in the oven with the chicken. Add it the last hour of baking. Use a covered casserole, twice as much water as rice, salt. That's it.

Serves 4 to 6.

OLD FASHIONED CHICKEN CASSEROLE

4- or 5-pound chicken or fowl

1 onion

1 cup thin cream or evaporated milk

Flour

Bread crumbs

Prepare chicken or fowl, cook until tender in 1 quart water, adding salt and pepper. Remove chicken. Cool. Remove meat from bones, saving all skin, bones, and fat. Keep the meat in fairly large pieces.

Simmer these along with the onion in the liquid in which chicken was cooked; allow to simmer until liquid looks to be about half of what you started with. Remove from heat. Strain. Add 1 cup thin cream or evaporated milk. Mix 4 tablespoons flour with cold water so it is runny, add slowly to liquid. Cook over low heat stirring constantly until thickened. Season to taste.

Use a good-sized casserole. Place chicken pieces on a layer of bread crumbs. Pour sauce over all. Top with buttered crumbs. Bake at 350 degrees for 45 minutes.

Serves 8.

SEARSPORT CHICKEN PIE [A PERIOD PIECE]

FILLING

3 cups cooked chicken, cut in large pieces

1 can cream of mushroom soup, undiluted

1 pimento, diced fine

CRUST

2 cups sifted flour

1 teaspoon soda

2 teaspoons cream of tartar

½ teaspoon salt

½ cup vegetable shortening

1 egg

½ cup milk

Mix all together and heat mixture. If pimento is already diced in jar, use ¼ cup.

Sift dry ingredients together, work in shortening using a pastry blender. No blender? Then use 2 knives. Beat egg, combine with milk; add to dry mixture, using a fork for mixing. Divide mixture in half and roll out.

Turn pastry onto 10-inch pie plate. Roll out second pastry before filling lower crust with hot mixture. Fill bottom pastry with hot chicken filling. Cut 3 slits in top pastry, fit over hot filling, flute edges together.

Bake at 400 degrees for 18 minutes. Serve hot. It amazes me—this pie is always baked within the 18 minutes. Serve with mashed squash, cranberry sauce, and celery.

Serves 6.

CHICKEN SALAD

3 cups cooked chicken cut in large chunks

3 tablespoons lemon juice

1 cup halved seedless green grapes

1½ cups very thinly slivered celery

1 cup slivered toasted almonds

1 cup mayonnaise—if you prefer, Miracle Whip

¼ cup light cream or dairy sour cream

1 teaspoon dry mustard

Dash of black pepper

½ teaspoons alt

Dash of soy sauce

½ teaspoon curry powder

Nothing can be more of a showpiece for chicken than a large platter heaped high with this delicious way of preparing chicken salad. This is not a Maine recipe at all. A lot of people have retired in Maine from out-of-state; this is how the recipe came to us. It is sure to be one of your favorite ways of serving Maine chicken.

Prepare cooked chicken, marinate with fresh lemon juice. Place bowl in refrigerator while preparing dressing. Mix mayonnaise, cream, mustard, pepper, salt, as many dashes of soy sauce as you like, and the curry powder. Taste for seasoning.

Mix with the marinated chicken, add halved green grapes, slivered celery, and slivered almonds. Taste again for seasoning. Chill. Turn onto large platter on bed of lettuce, garnish with drained pineapple chunks, ripe olives, and paprika.

Serves 10.

CHICKEN A LA KING [A PERIOD PIECE]

4 tablespoons butter or margarine

1 cup sliced mushrooms

4 tablespoons flour

2 cups milk or chicken stock

½ teaspoon salt

¼ teaspoon pepper

2½ cups diced cooked chicken

1 cup frozen or canned peas

3 tablespoons diced pimento

Lightly brown mushrooms in butter or margarine. Blend in the flour. Gradually stir in the milk or chicken stock. Cook in top of double boiler, stirring until thickened. Add chicken, cooked peas and pimento. Season to taste and cook 10 minutes more. Serve in patty shells, toast cups, or on toast points.

Serves 8.

4 Meats

NEW ENGLAND BOILED DINNER

At the first sign of fall you hear Maine people talking about a boiled dinner. We make boiled dinner year-round nowadays, but when the new potatoes, carrots, cabbage, turnips, and beets are ready in the gardens, then you hear the remark, "We must have a boiled dinner."

We have other things in mind when cooking that dinner, too. There will be red flannel hash for later in in the week. There will be cold corned beef for sandwiches or to serve with baked potatoes. . . . We like gray corned beef in Maine, not red. We find many people who like to corn their own beef, too. That is understandable for not many storekeepers corn their own beef anymore. You have probably learned that the best corned beef is lightly corned and has not been in the brine too long.

These directions will help you if you want to corn your own piece of brisket or thick rib for that boiled dinner. If you ask your butcher to corn the beef, then 48 hours in the brine is about right.

TO CORN BEEF

Mix together two quarts cold water and 1 cup salt. Put the piece of fresh brisket or thick ribs into the brine and cover with a plate (inverted) to hold the beef under the brine. Allow beef to stay in the brine for about 48 hours.

In the past, cellars were cool and Maine housewives used their old stone crocks for corning beef. I suggest you use a large bowl and place the beef to corn in the refrigerator.

NEW ENGLAND BOILED DINNER

If you wish, the following seasonings may be added to the brine before placing beef in it:

- 3 tablespoons sugar
- 1 teaspoon black pepper
- 1 clove garlic
- 2 bay leaves
- 2 teaspoons mixed pickling spices

TO COOK BOILED DINNER

Rinse corned beef to remove the brine, place in a kettle large enough to hold beef and vegetables that are to be added later. If you do not have such a kettle, then cook the beef first, later removing it and adding the vegetables to cook in the liquid.

Keep in mind that corned beef is a tougher cut of meat and requires a long, slow cooking time to become tender. Add enough cold water so that it comes up about halfway around the corned beef. Cover the kettle, bring to a boiling point, reduce heat, and allow at least 1 hour per pound.

If you are Maine born, then you probably cook potatoes, carrots, cabbage, turnips, and beets in your boiled dinner. Many cooks add onions and parsnips.

NEW ENGLAND BOILED DINNER

The carrots and potatoes are pared and left whole, the turnip is pared and sliced and the slices cut in half if the turnip is large. The cabbage is quartered and outside leaves are discarded if need be.

Beets are not pared. Tops are cut down to within a half inch of the beets, the long slim root is left on to prevent beets from "bleeding", and they are cooked whole and in a separate covered saucepan. Often canned beets are used as they only need reheating.

About one hour before the corned beef is done, remove cover from kettle, put carrots, turnip, and cabbage in to cook, placing them down around the corned beef in the liquid. Cover kettle, bring back to steaming point, lower heat, and cook a half hour, then place pared potatoes in kettle, bring back to steaming point, then lower heat and cook until vegetables are tender.

Beets (cooked separately) should be ready when the boiled dinner is placed on your old ironstone platter.

Slice corned beef and arrange down center of platter, arrange the colorful vegetables around slices of beef, dotting the red beets on top of the vegetables for added color. A few sprigs of parsley go well here, too.

USE THE LEFTOVERS TO MAKE RED FLANNEL HASH

In Maine our red flannel hash is a vegetable hash. We like the cold corned beef sliced and served with the hot hash, especially with hot biscuits. Try chopping

NEW ENGLAND BOILED DINNER

your leftover vegetables after dinner. They store more easily in your refrigerator and you will notice less odor from them.

Chop all the leftover vegetables together, including the beets, making them as fine as your family likes. Add some fat and liquid left from cooking the dinner. Mix well, season with salt and pepper to taste. Store in refrigerator.

When ready to cook, turn into baking dish and bake at 350 degrees for one hour. If you prefer, get out your heavy black spider and fry hash slowly, taking care that it does not burn.

STIFLED BEEF

- 2 pounds top or bottom of round, cut into serving pieces or chuck cut for stew beef
- Flour, salt, and pepper
- 4 tablespoons fat
- 2 cups cold water

In Maine it is called stifled beef, although you may call it smothered beef. It is served with mashed or baked potatoes. It is a hearty, satisfying meal. It is also a way of making a tougher cut of beef very tender from long slow cooking.

Using a paper bag, put about 1 cup flour in it. Add salt and pepper. Shake. Put beef in bag and shake so each piece is coated. Brown in melted fat in frying pan.

Remove meat to covered casserole. Add another ¼ cup of flour from bag to fat in pan, stir to blend, add cold water slowly. Bring to boiling point, stir and thicken.

Pour over beef. Cover. Bake at 350 degrees for at least 2 hours or until beef is tender. Any leftovers may be used in making a beef pie.

Serves 6.

OLD AMERICAN CHOP SUEY [A PERIOD PIECE]

1 onion

3 tablespoons margarine or butter

1½ pounds hamburg

1½ cups elbow macaroni

2 cans tomato soup*

*If you prefer, in place of 2 cans of tomato soup, use 1 No. 2½ can tomatoes, 1 small can tomato paste, pinch oregano, 1 bay leaf, ½ teaspoon celery seed.

Saute 3 slices of onion in 3 tablespoons margarine or butter. When onion is soft, add 1½ pounds hamburg and cook over medium heat until red color has left. Add and salt and pepper to this.

In the meantime, cook elbow macaroni. Put about 1½ quarts water in covered pan. Bring to a boil. Add salt. Add 1½ cups dry elbow macaroni. Stir and bring to full, rolling boil on high heat. Stir constantly and boil for 2 minutes on high. Then, cover pan. (No boiling over when done in this manner,) At end of 10 minutes, remove cover, stir and put in colander to drain.

Back to hamburg, add 2 cans tomato soup*, undiluted, mix well. Add drained, cooked elbow macaroni. No other seasoning needed. Turn into 2-quart casserole.

Bake at 325 degrees for 45 minutes or until bubbly. Sprinkle top with grated Parmesan cheese, if desired.

Serves 6.

SCALLOPED POTATOES AND BOLOGNA [A PERIOD PIECE]

I have a strong feeling about this recipe. It was in the first column I ever wrote and has been one of the most popular recipes I have used.

4 cups thinly sliced raw Maine potatoes

1 cup thinly sliced raw peeled onions

2 cups medium white sauce

Salt and pepper

½ to 1 pound bologna

Cook thinly sliced potato and onion together in boiling salted water (only about ½ cup) for 10 minutes. Drain.

Prepare 2 cups medium white sauce (see below).

Cut ½ to 1 pound bologna into cubes. Use a buttered 2-quart casserole. Arrange a layer of drained cooked potato and onion slices in casserole. Season. Place cubes of bologna all over this. Pour medium white sauce over bologna. Then place layer of potato and onion and bologna, ending with the white sauce.

Bake uncovered at 375 degrees for 45 minutes.

Serves 4.

SCALLOPED POTATOES AND BOLOGNA [A PERIOD PIECE]

4 tablespoons margarine or butter

4 tablespoons flour

½ teaspoon salt

Bit of pepper

2 cups milk

MEDIUM WHITE SAUCE

In a saucepan over medium heat melt margarine or butter. Add flour. Add salt and pepper. Add milk, slowly, stirring constantly until thickened.

BASIC SAUSAGE

There are many people in Maine who make their own sausage meat. If you have this in mind, then this basic rule will be of help to you. Watch for fresh pork specials in your market, using a less expensive cut of pork such as a pork shoulder. Ask your meat man to grind this for you or do it yourself, putting it through your food grinder.

9 pounds fresh lean pork

2 tablespoons sage or thyme

1 teaspoon red pepper

¼ cup salt

2 tablespoons black pepper

Put 9 pounds fresh, lean pork through meat grinder. Blend with sage or thyme. Add red pepper, salt, and black pepper. Mix well and make patties or pack into covered containers. Freeze or store in refrigerator for a short time.

SLUMGULLION

Slumgullion . . . . comes from the long-time friend who has contributed many recipes to my "Cooking Down East" column. I will say this is one of the most popular recipes I have ever used.

2 pounds stew beef

4 onions

1 large can tomatoes; if home canned, 1 quart

1 teaspoon poultry seasoning

Salt to taste

Cut stew beef into about 1-inch cubes. Do not brown. Place in a 2-quart casserole. Cover with sliced onions. Salt the onions. Turn canned tomatoes over onions, add another sprinkle of salt and 1 teaspoon poultry seasoning.

Cover pan; use foil if no cover available. Bake at 275 or 300 degrees for about 3 hours.

In the meantime, combine ⅓ cup flour with ½ cup cold water, mix and allow to stand—this prevents lumping when stirred into hot beef mixture.

When meat is tender, stir in the flour mixture; this thickens the slumgullion immediately. Serve with mashed potatoes or on cooked noodles. Freezes well. Use a double boiler to thaw and reheat.

Serves 6 to 8.

UNITY BEEF CASSEROLE [A PERIOD PIECE]

This recipe is referred to as "the most used casserole in Unity," and that is the kind of recipe we like. The amount yields two good sized casseroles, one for giving and one for home use; or you could freeze one, if you liked.

1½ pounds ground beef

1 medium onion, diced

3 tablespoons butter or margarine

2 cans cream of mushroom soup

1½ cups milk

½ pound package medium noodles, cooked

½ pound American cheese shredded

Buttered crumbs

Cook onion in about 3 tablespoons margarine. Add ground beef and cook until brown. Mix soup and milk together and add to meat. Cook and drain noodles, then add. Add shredded cheese and mix well.

Turn into 2 buttered casseroles. Top with buttered crumbs. Bake ½ hour at 350 degrees.

Serves 6 to 8.

SCALLOPED HAM AND POTATOES

- 5 cups thinly sliced, pared raw potatoes
- 3 cups diced, cooked ham
- 1 cup thinly sliced onions
- 3 cups thin white sauce

Arrange potatoes, ham, and onion in alternate layers in a casserole. Pour the white sauce over all.

Cover and bake at 375 degrees for one hour. Remove cover and bake 30 minutes longer or until potatoes are tender.

Serves 6.

- 3 tablespoons margarine or butter
- 3 tablespoons flour
- Dash of black pepper
- 1½ teaspoons salt
- 3 cups milk

THIN WHITE SAUCE

In a saucepan melt margarine or butter over low heat. Stir in flour, salt, and pepper. Add milk gradually, continue to stir and cook over low until sauce thickens.

5 Eggs and Cheese

If you lived on a farm, there probably was a flock of hens. My uncle had a flock which took care of our needs but he also sold eggs. I remember him preparing the smoothly worn wooden egg box with its layers of eggs for the trip to the village once a week.

Usually I went along, for I liked the wagon ride with Old Nell. The Board Road to town now has been discontinued, for it would take you right up through the Brunswick Naval Air Station. Then it took you up through the bogs and the Brunswick Plains.

STUFFED EGGS

You may call them stuffed or deviled eggs, probably you remember them as one of the first picnic foods in your family. Whether you take them on a picnic or serve them at home with potato salad on a hot summer night they are sure to be popular.

6 hard-cooked eggs, shelled

¼ teaspoon salt

Dash of pepper

¼ teaspoon dry mustard

4 tablespoons mayonnaise

Few drops onion juice

Cut the shelled, hard-cooked eggs in halves lengthwise; remove yolks, lay whites aside. Mash yolks using a fork, add remaining ingredients. Refill whites with this mixture, rounding the filling.

Stuffed eggs may have all sorts of seasonings added. One favorite at our house is to add just a small can of deviled ham and mayonnaise, nothing else.

If you are going on a picnic, they may be leveled off and two put together for easier carrying.

MAINE EGG CASSEROLE [A PERIOD PIECE]

A stuffed casserole is asked for again and again by a men's group that meets on Mondays in the Augusta area. There is every reason in the world for calling it Maine Egg Casserole.

Allowing 3 halves of stuffed egg per person, use the number of eggs required for your family. Fill egg halves according to previous recipe.

Place in buttered shallow glass baking dish. Pour cheese sauce over stuffed eggs, so that sauce comes up around them. Top with buttered crumbs. Bake at 400 degrees for 20 minutes.

For 8 eggs, use 2 cups cheese sauce:

4 tablespoons margarine

4 tablespoons flour

½ teaspoon salt

¼ teaspoon pepper

2 cups milk

2 cups cut-up cheese, your choice

TO MAKE THE CHEESE SAUCE

Mix all ingredients except the cheese and cook over medium heat until thickened. Stir in cheese and continue stirring until cheese is fully melted. This will make more than 2 cups sauce once cheese is added.

WELSH RABBIT

We talk about making a rarebit in Maine by using a cream sauce and adding cut-up cheese. It is good, but not nearly as good as this recipe. This one is thickened by eggs and cheese, only. Try it for a true Welsh rabbit.

1 tablespoon butter

1 pound cheese

Dash red pepper

½ teaspoons alt

¼ teaspoon black pepper

1 tablespoon Worcestershire Sauce

½ teaspoon dry mustard

1 cup milk

2 eggs

Use a double boiler. Melt butter and add cheese that has been cut into small pieces. Stir butter and cheese together, but do not become alarmed when the cheese becomes stringy, it will eventually all become smooth.

Once the cheese had started to melt, add the milk gradually, continuing to stir. Mix the seasonings together, then add to the butter, cheese, and milk mixture.

Beat eggs slightly in a bowl. Pour some of the cheese mixture into it and mix together. Then pour this all into the top part of the double boiler. Continue to stir and add the rest of the cheese mixture. You will find that once the eggs have been added the entire mixture suddenly smooths out. Continue to stir until the mixture is thick enough to serve on toast or crackers.

SWISS CHEESE PIE

Cheese pie is another way of designating quiche—this recipe is recognizably a Quiche Lorraine. Ironically, within about ten years of *Cooking Down East*'s publication, quiche became very common, and was often associated with women and luncheons and definitely not menfolk eating heartily.

Cheese pie for breakfast would have been a 'natural' years ago, when our menfolk ate heartier breakfasts than they do now. It is still a good idea, although it would be better if served for lunch or supper.

Pastry to line a 10-inch pie plate (line the pan with pastry and chill while you make the filling.)

4 eggs

2 cups thin or thick cream or milk

1 cup grated Swiss cheese

¾ teaspoon salt

6 bacon slices

Cook bacon, break in bits. Grate cheese. If the very last will not grate, merely add bits to make cupful. Beat eggs slightly. Add milk and seasonings. Take pie plate from refrigerator, spread soft butter over bottom of unbaked crust.

Sprinkle cooked crumbled bacon all over crust. Sprinkle grated cheese over bacon. Pour in the egg and milk mixture.

Bake at 425 degrees for 15 minutes. Then lower temperature to 300 degrees and bake 40 minutes longer or until you test with a

SWISS CHEESE PIE

Pinch nutmeg

Pinch cayenne pepper

Pinch sugar

1/8 teaspoon black pepper

1 tablespoon soft butter

silver knife and it comes out clean. Serve hot or warm.

Serves 6.

EGG PANCAKE

Egg pancake . . . looks like a glorified popover. This recipe did not come from our family, but it is an old-fashioned recipe and came from down along the New Meadows River, too.

2 eggs well beaten

½ cup milk

⅓ cup sifted flour

¼ teaspoon salt

Beat ingredients together in order given. Heat a 9-inch skillet, using 2 tablespoons shortening. If you have a heavy black spider, do use it, for you are going to slide this egg pancake into the oven shortly.

Pour batter into skillet. Allow to cook on top of stove for a minute or two. Then place pan in 425-degree oven and bake for 15 to 25 minutes until "popped" and golden brown. Serve hot with pats of butter or crispy bacon.

Keep in mind, a heavy black frypan absorbs heat faster and the egg pancake will cook more quickly in it. The length of time will depend on the kind of pan used. Remember too, some pans cannot go into the oven because of their handle.

FRIDAY SANDWICH FILLING

People speak about store cheese, rat cheese, and mouse-trap cheese. Actually, they are referring to aged cheddar cheese. This sandwich filling comes from Camden and it was recommended that store cheese be used. The seasonings can be adapted to suit the tastes of your family. This is a hearty sandwich and I like its name.

3 hard cooked eggs

1 cup cut-up store cheese

1 small green pepper

Salad dressing or mayonnaise to mix

1 teaspoon horseradish

Salt to taste

These ingredients may all be put through a food grinder, using a coarse blade. Or, in the good old Maine way, you could get out your wooden bowl and chopping knife and chop these ingredients fine. After chopping or grinding, add the mayonnaise, horse radish, and salt, seasoning to suit your family's taste.

CHEESE CRUNCHIES

This recipe appeared a few years ago under the name Cheddar Crisps in the now-defunct* Gourmet *magazine, where a friend of mine found it, tried it, and served the Crunchies at a party. I liked them so much that I asked for the recipe and have since made it often, especially around the holidays. Without knowing that the Crunchies ever appeared in a book by Marjorie Standish, I put the recipe in my* Bangor Daily News *column, "Taste Buds," and subsequently in my book,* Maine Home Cooking. *I use butter, not margarine, and the sharpest cheddar I can find but no onion salt. I form them into logs, chill them, and slice off thin slices to bake on a cookie sheet.

2 cups grated sharp cheese

2 sticks margarine, at room temperature

2 cups rice crispies

2 cups sifted flour

Dash of red pepper

½ teaspoon onion salt

You'll notice there are no eggs, which is correct. The first time I made these I grated the cheese, which is not necessary. Buy it all grated.

Mix all ingredients together, chill dough. Form into balls and flatten on ungreased cookie sheet. Bake at 400 degrees for about ten minutes.

MACARONI CASSEROLE [A PERIOD PIECE]

This is another Aroostook County recipe. You will like everything about it, including the fact this is uncooked macaroni mixed with the ingredients. All the ingredients are mixed together, turned into the casserole, refrigerated 8 to 24 hours, then baked.

2 cups uncooked elbow macaroni

2 cans cream of mushroom soup

4 ounces dried beef—less than this may be used

1½ cups cheddar cheese, cubed

4 hard-cooked eggs, diced

¼ cup minced onion

2 cups milk

No seasoning needed

Combine all ingredients, turn into 2-quart casserole. Cover and refrigerate overnight, or for at least 8 hours. This, of course, allows the uncooked macaroni to soften before baking.

Bring to room temperature and baked uncovered at 350 degrees for one hour.

Serves 6, generously.

6 Vegetables

In this chapter I have tried to include your favorite ways of cooking potatoes. But it is just as important to talk about Maine baked beans, dandelion greens, or fiddleheads, for they are longtime favorites in Maine. The other recipes are popular ones that all have appeared in "Cooking Down East" columns.

MAINE BAKED BEANS

1 pound dry beans (2 cups)

2 tablespoons granulated sugar

1 teaspoon salt

Few grains of black pepper

½ teaspoon dry mustard

2 tablespoons molasses

½ pound salt pork

About 2½ cups boiling water

Pick over the dry beans. Wash them. Place in a good-sized bowl. Cover with cold water and allow to soak overnight.

In the morning, drain beans. Place in a beanpot. Mix all seasonings together in small bowl. Turn into beanpot on top of soaked, drained beans and mix altogether until all beans are coated with seasonings. Be careful not to add too much molasses, it can cause beans to harden as they bake.

Add boiling water, about 2½ cups, or enough to cover beans in pot. Score salt pork by making gashes in it. Wash pork in hot water. Place it on top of beans. Cover beanpot. Beans are now ready to go into oven.

A low temperature is needed, around 250 degrees for 8 hours of baking, and they should not be stirred but do need attention occasionally, for they need to be kept covered with boiling water at all times. The beanpot itself needs to be kept covered until the last hour of baking, then remove cover so the beans will brown.

MAINE BAKED BEANS

Forgot to soak your beans? Never mind. In the morning, parboil them in water to cover, just until skins wrinkle. I never parboil beans unless I forget to soak them, just overnight soaking is enough.

Pour over beef. Cover. Bake at 350 degrees for at least 2 hours or until beef is tender. Any

MAINE DANDELION GREENS

Digging dandelion greens in Maine has been going on for generations. Everyone uses a case knife, a flat-type kitchen knife for digging. You can spot the old-timers, they carry bushel baskets . . . . many Maine families make a dinner of salt pork, boiled potatoes, and dandelion greens.

If yours is a big "mess" of greens then you will use 1 pound of salt pork. Try to get pork with layers of lean, it adds such flavor. Slice pork into four thick pieces, score them.

Put the pork to cook in a good-sized pan with about a quart of water. Cover kettle, bring to steaming point, lower heat, and cook slowly about one hour. It is a good idea to start cooking salt pork about 2½ to 3 hours before dinner is ready.

About 1½ hours before dinnertime, drain the well washed greens and place them in the kettle with the salt pork. Cover and bring back to a boil. I like to stir the greens and pork around so that the pork is distributed through the greens for good flavor. Make certain the greens do not stick to the pan. Allow greens and pork to cook for 1 hour.

A half-hour before dinner time the pared potatoes should be added. Place pared potatoes down into the greens. This insures their turning green and taking on the delicious flavor of pork and greens. I like to pepper the potatoes, usually there is enough salt from the pork so they do not need more added, but that can come later if you do need it.

Cover kettle, bring back to steaming point, lower heat and cook until potatoes are tender, which takes about one-half hour.

MAINE DANDELION GREENS

Have a large platter ready, heap the drained dandelions on it. Surround the greens with boiled potatoes. Sprinkle paprika on the potatoes. Lay the tender strips of salt pork on the greens. Use a dash of paprika on these, too.

Now it's time to call the family to dinner!

FIDDLEHEADS

Gather fiddleheads before they grow too tall—from two to six inches. Merely break them off and put them in your sack or basket. Fiddleheads you gather or buy will need cleaning to rid them of the brown flecks. If you tap them gently or shake them, this will drop off. Then give them a good washing and you are ready to cook them.

Place well-washed fiddleheads in a saucepan. Add about a half-inch cold water. Salt the greens. Place cover on pan, bring to steaming point on a high heat. Lower the heat and cook for 5 to 10 minutes. Check with a fork for doneness. Never cook fiddleheads over 10 minutes, for if you do they will be slimy! (There's just no other way to express the state they will be in.)

Drain greens, season with salt, pepper, and butter. They are now ready for serving. Because of the delicate flavor of fiddleheads, I think you will agree they taste best when served just plain.

SKILLET CREAMED POTATOES

Mrs. Standish considered potatoes a vegetable."When we talk about vegetables we have one thing in mind—Maine potatoes," she wrote in Cooking Down East. *She recommended a visit to Aroostook County when they were in bloom, describing the fields of potatoes as a breath-taking sight. She included many favorite potato recipes, eight of them plus sixteen other vegetable recipes. In* Keep Cooking the Maine Way *she added three more to the repertoire. Altogether her potato recipes usually added milk, cheese, or cream to make a sauce in which the potatoes were cooked, lots of times finished in an oven as a casserole.*

4 cups raw potatoes, cut in ½-inch squares

2 cups top milk or light cream

1 teaspoon salt

¼ teaspoon black pepper

Use a heavy skillet and a cover. Put diced, raw potatoes in skillet, add cream, salt, and pepper. Cover. Simmer over low heat for 30 minutes or until potatoes are tender, stirring now and then with a fork.

Serves 4 to 6.

FRESH SHELL BEANS

Shell beans are a gift from the garden, rarely found in grocery stores, and only occasionally at farmer's markets. I learned about Maine shell beans from a Maine-born neighbor when I first moved here about 28 years ago and I have grown them every year since. Taylor's Horticultural Beans are the variety name I like, and I dedicate a couple fifteen foot rows to them. Pick when the pods are still soft, but flaccid, shell out, and eat right away and freeze some for winter, too.

Standish suggests that Mainers ate more shell beans than anyone else, but she did not consider Southerners who grow "shelly beans" plentifully and eat them. Interestingly also, she refers to "sauce" dishes. In early America it was common for people to refer to vegetables as "garden sauce." The small bowls, smaller than soup size, were how vegetables were served and got their names from the term "sauce" for vegetables.

Using about 1 cup cold water to 3 cups shelled beans, add salt, cover pan, bring to steaming point; lower heat and cook for at least 40 minutes, or until tender. Hopefully, the water will be mostly absorbed. Take care they do not burn. Add a little milk or cream, salt, pepper, and butter. Serve in sauce dishes.

FRESH SHELL BEANS

If you have ever looked for the directions for cooking shell beans, then you will appreciate finding them here. It could be that in Maine we cook more shell beans than anywhere else. If we have making Maine succotash in mind, we have to cook the shell beans first.

MAINE SUCCOTASH

In some parts of the country, succotash is made by combining corn cut from the cob with lima beans. It just so happens that in Maine we combine cooked corn cut from the cob with cooked shell beans. Add cream or milk, a piece of butter, and salt and pepper to taste.

Try combining a can of cream style corn with one can of shell beans in top of double boiler, add a little cream or milk, a piece of butter, salt and pepper. Serve in sauce dishes. This is a good vegetable to serve with meat loaf and baked potatoes.

STEWED BEANS

Whether you call them stewed beans or live in the North Country and have always referred to them as Bean Swagin—pronounced Sway-gin—this favorite Maine food was popular with lumberjacks. It was served with johnnycake. For generations cooks have handed down this way of preparing a food that "sticks to the ribs." There are old-time cooks who could say, "Never fry the salt pork, just put the pork and beans on to boil together." Either way, it is a delicious meal.

Pick over one quart dry beans, wash and soak overnight. You will probably choose yellow eye beans, since they will be similar to the old fashioned beans of long ago. In the morning, drain beans, put in kettle and cover with boiling water.

Wash ½ pound salt pork and place in kettle. Or, as some cooks prefer, slice pork, then brown in frypan before adding to beans. Cover kettle, bring to steaming point; cook slowly for 4 to 5 hours or, as you might hear a cook say, "Until they are all chowdered up."

Stir occasionally. To keep from burning, you may need to add more water as they cook. Season with pepper before dishing up. If the pork does not season enough, add salt. Either hot biscuits or big hot squares of johnnycake will be delicious with the stewed beans.

CORN CASSEROLE

This corn casserole, or corn pudding as it is sometimes called, was a favorite food when as 'boarders' we gathered around the Burnham table in Bridgton years ago. Mrs. Burnham cooked and served this in her heavy black spider. If you do not own one, then prepare in a fry pan and turn mixture into a casserole for baking.

2 tablespoons margarine or butter

1 small onion

2 tablespoons flour

2 cups milk

Salt and pepper to taste

1 can cream style corn (2 cups)

2 eggs beaten

Buttered crumbs for topping.

Melt margarine or butter in fry pan, dice onions, cook in melted fat until soft. Mix in flour, salt and pepper, add milk slowly, stirring and cooking over low heat until thickened. Add corn, mix well, remove from heat; add to beaten eggs, combine carefully, turn into buttered casserole. Top with buttered crumbs.

Set casserole in pan with hot water. Bake at 350 degrees for 45 minutes.

Serves 6.

MOCK LOBSTER SANDWICH [A PERIOD PIECE]

In case you are wondering how a recipe for mock lobster sandwich got into a chapter on vegetables, I think you should hear a little story. A few years back, I used this recipe in my column, after having it in a file for a few years before that. I found it was met with great enthusiasm. One woman wrote to tell me it is probably the very best recipe I have ever used in any column, so I could hardly leave it out of this cookbook, could I?

2 slices bread

Spread one slice with deviled ham. Slice a smallish cucumber lengthwise and place on deviled ham.

On other slice of bread, place sliced peeled tomato. Dab mayonnaise on tomato slices.

Put sandwich together and enjoy!

FRIED ZUCCHINI SLICES

The introduction of summer squash many years ago to Maine people brought a whole new idea about squash cookery. Of course, it was a whole new kind of squash. In more recent years, Maine cooks have become acquainted with zucchini squash. After all, you do not need to pare these . . . it makes for easier cooking.

It is best to choose summer squash or zucchini that has not grown too large . . . If you grow your own, then you will have to share your squashes, for nothing grows as fast as these two kinds of squash.

Use sufficient oil to cover surface of fry pan. Prepare slices about a half hour ahead by slicing unpared squash in ¼-inch slices, sprinkle with salt, spread on paper towel, allow to stand a half hour. This draws out the water from the squash so it may be fried without spattering.

When drained, place in a paper bag with sufficient flour to coat. Beat one or two eggs, depending upon amount of squash you are frying, dip each piece of floured squash into egg, and fry in hot oil. Turn until lightly browned. Remove and drain on paper towel. Good hot or cold. Salt is the only seasoning needed.

BAKED ACORN SQUASH

A long time ago when I worked for the power company in Bridgeton, there was The Teakettle Tea Room. It was a delightful place to eat. There they served acorn squash done in this way.

Wash the squash, cut in half lengthwise, remove seeds using a spoon. Wash once more, turn squash upside-down in a baking pan, pour ¼ inch cold water in pan.

Bake at 400 degrees for ½ hour. Remove from oven, turn squash right side up. Salt and pepper it, sprinkle with brown sugar (maple syrup is good, too). Place piece of butter in each half. Return to oven, bake 30 minutes longer. Serve.

7 Salads

Before the 1800s, there was a tradition of eating green salads adorned with cold cooked food, pickles, boiled eggs, even edible flowers. This practice was abandoned in the 1800s, partly due to concern for the "digestibility" of raw vegetables. Most cookbooks of the era that provided recipes for salad almost always mentioned cold cooked meat salads of chicken, lobster, or other leftover meat; cold cooked vegetables like asparagus or cauliflower, and potatoes, plus cole slaw, celery, and occasionally lettuce.

When Mrs. Standish was born around 1907, gelatin salads had not taken hold, even though Jello had come on the market about ten years before. During her life, the now-much-deplored sugary gelatin salad flourished and began its decline as she approached her late 80s. We ought not be surprised then, that her salads chapter is replete with gelatin salads.

She recalled cucumbers served with vinegar sprinkled on them and a little salt, still popular with Maine old-timers, and lettuce sprinkled with vinegar and sugar, even tomatoes sliced and sprinkled with sugar.

She remembered homemade mayonnaise, boiled dressing, which dated back into the 1800s, and tables set with cruets of oil and vinegar. Along with her peers, Mrs. Standish had to learn how to make a tossed salad, something that came a little belatedly to Maine from more sophisticated urban America. She reported on this in *Cooking Down East*:

"Along came tossed green salad. I learned about them the summer I worked for a retired couple at Old Orchard. They had traveled extensively and I learned a lot about food from them. They taught me to make green salads.

"Arriving home at the end of the summer, I offered to make a tossed green salad for my mother who had been asked to bring a salad to a public supper. That night I watched my large bowl of salad come down the long table. Across from me one woman asked another, 'What kind of a salad is this?' 'I don't know,' was the answer, 'but you're not going to like it.'"

In the spirit, then of Mrs. Standish's cookbooks, the salads you find here with the exception of Kennebec Salad will mostly be of the non-tossed variety.

TWO WEEK SALAD

Cabbage used in this manner may be called salad or a relish. This is especially good served with fish.

1 large head cabbage

1 large onion

¾ cup vinegar

1 cup sugar

1 teaspoon salt

¾ cup salad oil

Chop or grate together the head of cabbage and the large onion. Place in a large bowl.

In meantime, boil together the vinegar, oil, sugar (yes, this amount is correct) and salt.

Be sure that the chopped cabbage and onion are well mixed. Pour the boiling hot dressing over the vegetable mixture. Now, don't touch it. Just leave it as it is for 1½ hours, before mixing or tossing together.

Now mix and store in a covered container at least 12 hours before serving.

Serves 4 to 6.

MAINE LOBSTER SALAD

Allowing one boiled lobster per person, cut lobster meat into about 1-inch pieces. Add salt and pepper, mix with mayonnaise, serve on lettuce with a sprinkling of paprika. If you wish, try marinating cut-up lobster meat with lemon juice, allowing it to be refrigerated before mixing with mayonnaise. Some cooks even marinate the lobster meat with a small amount of oil dressing. Others add finely diced celery. Many cooks do not like to mask the flavor of lobster in any way, except with mayonnaise.

OLD-FASHIONED BOILED DRESSING

In case you have forgotten what zest old-fashioned boiled salad dressing can add to lobster salad this is a good place to use this recipe. It is delicious with many salads, like chicken.

3 tablespoons granulated sugar

2 teaspoons salt

2 teaspoons dry mustard

2 tablespoons flour

Dash cayenne pepper

2 eggs, slightly beaten

1½ cups milk

½ cup vinegar

2 tablespoons butter

Mix sugar, salt, dry mustard, flour, pepper, eggs, milk, and vinegar in the top part of a double boiler, set over boiling water, (Be sure you blend each ingredient as you add it.)

Stir mixture constantly until it becomes quite thick. Remove from over hot water. Add butter. Blend thoroughly. Cool. Makes 1 pint dressing.

WALDORF SALAD

It would be hard to recall when Waldorf salad was not popular in Maine. Do you remember it as a long ago favorite? It is a good salad to serve with pork.

2 cups diced unpared red apples

1 cup finely diced celery

½ cup coarsely cut walnuts

Mayonnaise or salad dressing to mix

Mix and serve on lettuce, sprinkling a few chopped nuts on top.

Serves 4 to 6.

FIVE CUP SALAD [A PERIOD PIECE]

The recipe for this easy-to-make salad appeared in Maine several years ago. Served on lettuce as a salad or in a sherbet glass as dessert you will find it good.

1 cup canned mandarin oranges

1 cup small marshmallows

½ cup flaked coconut

1 cup chunk-style pineapple

1 cup cultured soured cream

Mix all together after draining the fruit. Allow to stand, refrigerated, for 3 or 4 hours to blend the ingredients.

Serves 5.

FROZEN DATE SALAD [A PERIOD PIECE]

Back in 'cooking school days' frozen date salad appeared on one of the menus. It was one of the first frozen salads I remember and one of the best. Good for wintertime eating.

2 three-ounce packages cream cheese

2 cups cut dates

2 tablespoons orange juice

½ cup cream, whipped

Steam cut dates until soft in small amount water in saucepan. Cool. Soften cream cheese and combine with dates, orange juice, and whipped cream, turn into ice-cube tray and freeze. Serve with lettuce and mayonnaise.

Serves 12, as it is cut into small squares.

KENNEBEC SALAD

1 large head or 2 small heads lettuce

4 hard-cooked eggs

1 clove garlic

1 onion

1 teaspoon salt

3 tablespoons vinegar

Dash of Tabasco

½ cup salad oil

1 teaspoon dry mustard

¼ teaspoon pepper

Mash garlic in a salad bowl, then discard the garlic. Add salt, vinegar, Tabasco, salad oil, dry mustard, and pepper. Combine this dressing in the bowl, using a fork for mixing.

Slice onion into bowl, making very thin slices. Slice four hard-cooked eggs into bowl with onion. Mix these with the dressing.

Break lettuce into bowl, making about 2-inch pieces. Toss lightly in the dressing and serve.

Serves 8.

TEST OF TIME SALAD BOWL [A PERIOD PIECE]

1½ cups uncooked elbow macaroni

6 cups boiling water

3 teaspoons salt

8 frankfurters (1 pound)

½ cup well-seasoned French dressing (use bottled, if you wish)

2 tablespoons minced onion

3 teaspoons lemon juice

¼ cup diced celery

½ cup coarsely diced cucumber

2 tablespoons slivered green pepper

1 cup coarsely diced tomato

½ cup mayonnaise

Speck of black pepper

About ½ head shredded lettuce

Come summertime, Maine women try to come up with just the right idea for supper. Easy and different is the answer our Topsham friend has for us. She tells us that if the family has been blueberrying, then this is what they like to come home to. Because it has been their family favorite for years, it has an interesting name.

Cook macaroni in boiling salted water until tender. About 5 minutes before macaroni is done, add frankfurters. Cook 5 minutes longer, then drain. Remove franks and cut into bite-size pieces. Combine with drained macaroni.

Add French dressing, onion, and lemon juice. Chill all day or overnight or until mixture has a chance to mellow. Just before serving, toss with remaining ingredients, including the shredded lettuce. Add salt to taste.

Serves 8.

LEMON 'N' LIME SALAD

- 1 three-ounce package lemon gelatin
- 1 three-ounce package lime gelatin
- 2 cups boiling water
- 1 sixteen-ounce can crushed pineapple, undrained
- 1 cup evaporated milk
- 1 cup small curd cottage cheese
- 1 cup finely chopped pecans
- 1 tablespoon horse-radish
- 1 cup mayonnaise

Dissolve gelatin in boiling water. Add pineapple, stir to mix well. Place in refrigerator and chill until thickened.

Fold in cottage cheese; increase to 1½ cups if you prefer to omit nuts. Add evaporated milk, horse-radish, and mayonnaise. Turn into oiled mold. Chill. Turn onto a bed of endive. No dressing is needed—it is built into this salad.

Serves 12.

8 All Sorts of Bread

Mrs. Standish's mother's recipe for biscuits was pretty typical of late nineteenth century recipes for biscuits, and reveals the lingering use of older-style leavenings and measurements. The old ways of measuring were short-cuts for early cooks who didn't want to dig out a scale, but instead eye-balled the amounts. But they can baffle modern cooks. Here is a helping hand.

The best way to determine how much

shortening is the size of an egg, is to take an egg and some shortening and put them side-by-side, adding shortening until they look alike in volume. Or you can take an egg and lay it next to a stick of butter and observe that an egg is very close to four tablespoons or one-quarter cup.

To create leavening action, you need an acid and an alkali combined together to generate the gas trapped by gluten in flour which causes rising. Cream of tartar, still available in stores, and baking soda, which Mrs. Standish always designates as "soda," used together do the trick.

In some of the following recipes, you will see that Mrs. Standish calls for sour milk or buttermilk. Either provides enough acidity that a cook can use soda alone to develop enough rising action. Milk, off the farm in the early days, naturally soured into a very useful product. With pasteurization, the milk is essentially cooked, which prevents natural souring. You can sour milk by adding a bit of vinegar to promote light curdling.

Milk "to make a stiff batter" is merely enough to take up all the flour and hold the dough together sufficiently to handle it. Mrs. Standish watched her mother make biscuits and no doubt observed what the dough ought to look like when it was just right. You can get that experience by working with a recipe that precisely measures the milk, and will create a dough that you can observe for yourself. It is a blessed state to achieve when you have made biscuits so often that you can make them from scratch by eye.

MY MOTHER'S CREAM OF TARTAR BISCUITS

2 cups sifted flour

5 teaspoons cream of tartar

2 teaspoons soda

½ teaspoon salt

Piece of vegetable shortening, size of an egg

Milk—to make a stiff batter

Sift flour, soda, cream of tartar, and salt into a bowl. Cut in shortening, using a pastry blender or two knives. Add milk, using a fork to mix until just the last of the flour disappears and the dough seems just right for rolling and cutting into biscuits.

Turn dough onto lightly floured surface, handle very little, only enough to mold into shape and flatten by patting with your fingers or rolling to about 1-inch thickness

Dip biscuit cutter into flour and cut biscuits, placing on greased baking sheet. Place a dot of butter or margarine on each biscuit before putting into oven at 450 degrees for 10 to 12 minutes.

PERFECT BLUEBERRY MUFFINS

- 2 cups flour
- ½ teaspoon salt
- 3 teaspoons baking powder
- 1 cup milk
- 2 teaspoons lemon juice
- 1 well beaten egg
- ¼ cup salad oil
- ⅓ cup sugar
- ¾ cup blueberries

Sift flour, salt, baking powder, and sugar together. Beat egg well, add milk. Stir in oil and lemon juice.

Add milk, egg, and oil mixture to dry ingredients. Stir about 20 seconds. Flour should be all dampened, but mixture should still be lumpy. When just a few patches of flour are left, fold in blueberries, gently.

Fill greased muffin tins two-thirds full. Bake at 425 degrees for about 25 minutes.

GRAHAM GEMS

- 1½ cups graham flour
- 3 tablespoons sugar
- 1 teaspoon salt
- 1 teaspoon soda
- 3 tablespoons molasses
- 1 cup sour milk or buttermilk

Mix in order given. The graham flour is not sifted. Measure by spoonfuls into cup. Turn into mixing bowl. Add sugar, salt, and soda. Mix well, then add molasses and buttermilk or sour milk.

There are no eggs in this recipe. Turn into gem pans or muffin tins. Bake at 400 degrees for about 25 minutes.

SHREDDED WHEAT BREAD

2 cups boiling water

2 shredded wheat biscuits

2 tablespoons shortening

2 teaspoons salt

⅓ cup molasses

1 yeast cake

¼ cup lukewarm water

About 5 cups flour, unsifted

Measure water, shortening, salt, and molasses into mixing bowl, crumble shredded wheat into this. Dissolve yeast cake in warm water, then add to mixture when it has cooled to lukewarm.

Add flour by cupfuls, using as much as batter will take, until you have a stiff dough. Knead for 8 minutes. Grease bowl, place dough in it, let rise for 2 hours, covered.

Punch down the dough, then let rise another hour. Turn out on floured board, whack down, let relax for 10 minutes. Make into 2 loaves, place in greased pans, let rise until doubled.

Bake at 400 for 50 minutes. Turn onto rack, brush tops with butter, then cool and store.

STEAMED BROWN BREAD

If you are using your oven for baking beans in Saturday, then you could steam brown bread in the oven at the same time. You will like this recipe for in it you may use sour milk, buttermilk, water or regular milk."

1 cup rye meal

1 cup corn meal

1 cup graham flour

2 teaspoons soda

1 teaspoon salt

¾ cup molasses

2 cups sour milk or 2 cups buttermilk, or 1⅞ cup water or regular milk

Mix and sift dry ingredients (it is easier just to stir in the graham flour). Add molasses and milk, mix until well blended. Turn into greased pans or cans, do not fill more than two-thirds full.

You may steam this brown bread on top of the stove or in the oven. Cover the container of batter and set in a pan of water, being careful you do not have so much water it could boil over. Place in oven and let steam for 4 hours while the beans bake. If your cans have no cover, tie aluminum foil over the tops.

I always used to make a big thing of cutting the hot brown bread by looping a string around it and pulling the ends. It is a very old fashioned method but it works.

POPOVERS

In this popover recipe, Mrs. Standish says, "if the fuel you use means a preheated oven," in all likelihood, she is referring to a wood- or coal-heated cook stove, which does not come up to temperature as quickly as a gas or electric oven would. This means that in her day a good many Maine kitchens were still equipped with old-fashioned cooking stoves, and also explains why part of Mrs. Standish's career was spent demonstrating cookery to cooks who were switching to electric appliances.

2 eggs

⅞ cup milk

1 cup flour

¼ teaspoon salt

½ teaspoon melted butter

Sift flour, measure, sift with salt. Beat eggs slightly, add milk and butter. Add to flour mixing to make a smooth batter. Fill cold greased custard cups half full. Place cups on cookie sheet. Place in cold oven, set temperature at 400, bake for 50 minutes. If the fuel you use means a preheated oven, then 45 minutes for 400 is good.

This recipe makes 6 huge popovers.

DATE AND NUT BREAD

In my old, used copy of Cooking Down East, the pages that are splashed and spattered the most with cooking stains are in the baking and desserts chapters, which points to the original owner's constant use of Mrs. Standish's recipes on those pages, which include Banana Bread, Lemon Bread, Date and Nut Bread, and Diced Apple Bread; and it is anyone's guess which recipe the cook so often turned to. I am going to bet on Date and Nut Bread because a few years ago I asked readers of my column in the Bangor Daily News for a recipe for Date Nut Bread and ended up with lots of recipes for what was apparently a popular quick bread.

¾ cups chopped nuts

1 cup dates, chopped in pieces

1½ teaspoons soda

½ teaspoon salt

3 tablespoons shortening

¾ cup boiling water

2 eggs

1 teaspoon vanilla

1 cup sugar

1½ cups sifted flour

Mix the nuts, dates, soda, and salt together with a fork. Add shortening and boiling water. Mix well and allow to stand for 20 minutes.

Beat 2 eggs in large bowl with a fork. Add vanilla, sugar, and flour beating with a fork. Add date mixture, mixing enough to blend. Pour into greased 9 x 5 x 3-inch loaf pan. Bake at 350 degrees for 1 hour and 5 minutes, or until done.

PHILBROOK FARM DARK BREAD

"One winter a number of years ago," wrote Mrs. Standish, "this bread was introduced for teas at the Blaine House in Augusta. The recipe is still used for it proved to be very popular with guests." Philbrook Farm Inn in Shelburne, New Hampshire, was, and still is, famous for its New England home cooking. The town is on the Androscoggin River, and the recipe must have floated down stream washed ashore somewhere in Maine.

1½ cups graham flour

2 cups flour

2 teaspoons soda

½ teaspoon salt

½ cup brown sugar

½ cup molasses

2 cups sour milk or buttermilk

Measure graham flour by spooning it into the cup (not sifting it). Turn into a large bowl.

Sift all-purpose flour, measure and sift together with soda, salt, and brown sugar (either light or dark). Mix with graham flour, lightly. Add molasses and milk. Stir. Turn into a well-greased loaf pan. Bake at 350 degrees or 1 hour to 1 hour 10 minutes. Turn onto rack to cool.

SNOWBALL DOUGHNUTS [AND HOMEMADE BISCUIT MIX]

To make your own biscuit mix, use 2 cups sifted all-purpose flour, 4 teaspoons baking powder, · teaspoon salt. Sift together ad cut in 2 tablespoons shortening. Or you can use package biscuit mix with equally excellent results.

2 cups biscuit mix

1 cup applesauce

1 egg

½ teaspoon nutmeg

Measure biscuit mix by spoonfuls into measuring cup. Turn into bowl, stir in nutmeg, add unbeaten egg and applesauce, mix all together.

Have hot fat ready. If you have a thermometer, use 375 degrees. Dip by small teaspoonfuls, fry in hot fat until evenly brown. They just about turn themselves as they fry.

Drain on paper towel. Have ½ cup confectioner's sugar ready in a brown, fresh paper bag. Allow doughnut balls to cool about 20 minutes, then shake up in bag to coat into snowballs. Serve with hot coffee.

Makes 12 to 18 Snowballs.

OATMEAL BREAD

This recipe for oatmeal bread has a bit of a twist. A cup of hot coffee is added to this yeast bread to give a bit of color and good flavor. A recipe from the coast of Maine—Rockland.

¾ cup boiling water

1 cup hot coffee

1 cup rolled oats or oatmeal

⅓ cup shortening

½ cup molasses

3 teaspoons salt

2 envelopes dry yeast

¼ cup lukewarm water

2 eggs slightly beaten

5½ cups sifted flour

Combine boiling water, hot coffee (which may be made with instant coffee), rolled oats, shortening, molasses, and salt. Cool to lukewarm.

Add yeast to lukewarm water, stir to dissolve and when first mixture is cooled to lukewarm, add yeast. Add slightly beaten eggs. Add flour gradually, stirring until dough will take no more of flour. Place in greased bowl. Cover. Place in refrigerator for 2 hours.

Shape chilled dough into 2 loaves. You could knead this dough if you wish before placing these loaves in pans, but it is not necessary. Let rise in a warm place, as you do all yeast products. This takes about 2 hours or until the loaves are doubled in size.

Bake 1 hour at 350 degrees. Turn onto rack to cool; while still hot brush tops with butter.

HOT CROSS BUNS

Remembering how one of the large display windows at the old Frost and Smith's Bakery Shop in Brunswick looked the morning of Good Friday long ago, I cannot help but share this nostalgic moment with you.

We just did not see Hot Cross Buns until that morning. All day long the freshly baked buns were placed in the window and all day long a steady line of customers came into the bake shop to buy their supply for supper from the display in the window—row upon row of Hot Cross Buns. Before the days of packaging, you gave your order and your rolls were placed in white paper bags, in half dozen, dozen or two dozen lots. Sometimes you ordered two to be placed in a small paper bag and you ate them as you walked up Maine Street.

Now you can make your own Hot Cross Buns for your family to enjoy during the Lenten season—or at any time of year. Another recipe from our friend who has shared so many with us.

Scald milk. Stir yeast into lukewarm water. Combine scalded milk with sugar, butter, and salt; then stir until dissolved and butter is melted. Add dissolved yeast. Add well-beaten egg, cinnamon, raisins, and currants. Measure flour into measuring cup by spoonfuls so it will not be packed down. Add as much flour as can be stirred into dough. Cover bowl, let rise in a warm place until doubled.

HOT CROSS BUNS

1 cup milk

¼ cup sugar

2 tablespoons butter

½ teaspoon salt

1 yeast cake or 1 envelope dry yeast

¼ cup lukewarm water

1 egg, well beaten

¼ teaspoon cinnamon

½ cup seedless raisins

¼ cup currants

If you wish, ½ cup finely shredded citron

3 cups flour (unsifted)

Turn onto a lightly floured board, knead a few times, break off dough, and form into buns. Have some melted butter ready and coat each bun lightly. Place buns in a greased pan or pans. Cover. Allow to rise until doubled in bulk. After placing buns in pan for rising, take kitchen scissors and gently snip a cross in top of each bun. This will make it easier to ice the cross after the buns have been baked and cooled slightly.

Bake at 375 degrees for 15 to 20 minutes.

To make icing: Use about ¾ cups confectioners' sugar, mixed with a little milk. Use a teaspoon to dribble the cross on top of each bun. These are best when served fragrant and warm.

Makes 2 dozen buns.

OLD FASHIONED STRAWBERRY SHORTCAKE

This is a case of "do as I say, not as I do," because this recipe is what you will do if you want a real old-fashioned strawberry shortcake. I use this recipe, for it is a real biscuit shortcake, but instead of making 2 big layers, I cut the rolled-out dough with my largest 3-inch cookie cutter, bake the shortcakes on a cookie sheet, and serve them in soup plates.

2 cups sifted flour

1 teaspoon soda

2 teaspoons cream of tartar

½ teaspoon salt

1 stick butter or margarine

1 egg

About ⅔ cup milk

1 quart strawberries

1 cup sugar

1 cup cream

Sift flour, measure and sift together with soda, cream of tartar, and salt—you could use 4 teaspoons baking powder if you do not have soda and cream of tartar.

Blend in butter or margarine, using pastry blender. Beat egg slightly, combine with milk, add all at once to dry ingredients. Stir with a fork. Toss dough onto lightly floured board. Divide in halves. Roll or pat very gently and place one half in a buttered 8-inch circular baking pan. Brush that half with melted butter. Place other half on top. Bake at 450 degrees until shortcake is delicately browned, about 12 to 15 minutes.

OLD FASHIONED STRAWBERRY SHORTCAKE

Crush 1 quart washed, hulled, and drained strawberries, add sugar. Whip 1 cup cream. When shortcake is baked, split it, place bottom half cut side up on a platter or large plate. Cover with crushed strawberries. Lay second half of shortcake cut side up on top. Cover with remainder of strawberries. Spoon on the cream. Top with whole strawberries. Serve at once, cut in pie-shaped wedges.

Serves 8.

OLD-FASHIONED BAKEWELL CREAM BISCUITS

"Now there is nothing new about Bakewell Cream which is a substitute for cream of tartar," wrote Mrs. Standish. "In Maine we use cream of tartar and soda for leavening agents in many of our recipes, particularly the old ones. It is a sort of heritage we pass along to others. . . . Finally I listened to enough Maine cooks tell me about how good it is to use Bakewell Cream in all recipes calling for cream of tartar. You see, they have been using it for years . . ." Bakewell Cream contains sodium pyrophosphate, a mineral acid, and cornstarch, so is not just cream of tartar.

4 cups sifted flour

4 teaspoons Bakewell Cream

2 teaspoons soda

1 teaspoon salt

½ cup shortening—use a vegetable shortening for these biscuits

1½ cups milk

Mix and sift flour, Bakewell Cream, soda, and salt. Add shortening and cut in, using pastry blender or 2 knives. Add milk all at once, stir quickly with a fork to make a soft dough. Turn onto a floured board, knead 5 or 6 times. Roll out ½-inch or more thick. Cut with biscuit cutter, place on ungreased cookie sheet. Top each biscuit with a little butter or milk. Bake at 475 degrees for 5 minutes, turn off heat and leave in oven until golden brown. If you prefer, bake at 450 for 12 to 15 minutes. These biscuits are extra high and light.

Makes 24 biscuits, but you may easily halve the recipe.

CHEESE AND BACON MUFFINS

Cheese and bacon muffins disappear "like mist before the sun" when they appear in the Coffee Shop at the Augusta General Hospital on Wednesday mornings. These muffins will provide a built-in breakfast and will be popular in your family.

1 egg

1 cup milk

1 cup sharp cheese, shredded

2 cups flour, sifted

1 teaspoon salt

¼ cup sugar

3 teaspoons baking powder

Fry ¼ to ⅓ pound bacon, depending upon its leaness, reserve ⅓ cup of the drippings, beat egg slightly, stir in milk, ⅓ cup bacon fat, and 1 cup shredded cheese. Set aside.

Sift together flour, salt, sugar, and baking powder. Stir into the egg mixture. Crumble the fried bacon and add to mixture. Spoon into greased muffin tins. Bake at 400 degrees for 18 to 20 minutes.

Makes 12 muffins.

GRIDDLE CAKES

It surprised me a little when, after my first cookbook, someone remarked, "You forgot griddle cakes." We will not do that this time.

1¼ cups sifted flour

2½ teaspoons baking powder

3 tablespoons sugar

½ teaspoon salt

1 egg beaten ¾ cup milk

3 tablespoons melted fat or vegetable oil

Sift flour, measure and sift with baking powder, sugar, and salt. Beat egg, combine with milk and melted fat or oil. Add to dry ingredients all at once, mix until smooth.

Drop batter from a tablespoon onto a hot griddle, which has been greased, or not, according to manufacturer's directions. Spread the cakes out lightly using the back of the spoon. Cook on one side until puffed, full of bubbles, and cooked on the edges. Turn and cook on the other side. Serve immediately.

Makes 8 to 10 cakes.

MOLASSES DOUGHNUTS

- ½ cup molasses
- ½ cup sugar
- 1 egg
- 2 tablespoons melted shortening
- 1½ teaspoons soda in
- 1 cup buttermilk
- 3½ cups sifted flour
- ½ teaspoon cinnamon
- ½ teaspoon ginger
- ½ teaspoon salt

Beat molasses, sugar, egg, and shortening. Dissolve soda in buttermilk, then add to egg mixture. Sift flour together with cinnamon, ginger, and salt, then stir into egg mixture.

Refrigerate dough in covered container overnight, as in directions for plain doughnuts. Proceed with frying just as the directions are given in that recipe, too.

Roll out dough on a floured board to ½-inch thickness and cut with floured doughnut cutter. Fry until golden brown in deep fat heated to 375 degrees. Turn doughnuts once. Drain on brown paper.

Makes 30 doughnuts.

9 Just Desserts

Mrs. Standish began her *Cooking Down East* dessert chapter with the brave claim that, "Maine cooks like to cream, to beat, and to bake from scratch, and as long as they do at least a remnant of good old Maine cooking will remain." She admitted, "True, mixes are in demand," but she liked that Maine cooks preferred doing it all themselves. She credited this to improved ingredients like flour and shortening, which in her time meant the hydrogenated vegetable oils that we now view skeptically.

Mrs. Standish' education as a home economist also meant she was a hearty believer in exact measurement and precise directions: "'Flour to make a stiff batter'" and "'Bake until done'" worked well years ago, but definite amounts, temperatures, and time are far easier and give greater confidence." Surely, precision worked with standardization of ingredients. We can go to the store and come home with ingredients that are exactly the same as the last time we acquired them while in the past flour from a local mill varied with the amount of moisture in the local wheat, the sharpness of the millstones, and the speed of the water wheel. Butter varied in fat content, and the texture of sugar scraped from a loaf varied according to the cook's hand. Ingredients like that required observation, experience, and judgement from the baker.

And a gas or electric stove, like the ones Mrs. Standish professionally taught the use of, with a calibrated thermostat, will reliably maintain a given temperature over the required time to bake, unlike the much more variable wood- or coal-burning cook stoves that Mrs. Standish fondly remembered from her childhood. "Enough" and "Done" was learned by the young cooking alongside experienced elders.

MELT-IN-YOUR-MOUTH BLUEBERRY CAKE

"Taken from one of our Maine church cookbooks, it is undoubtedly the most popular recipe ever used in my column," wrote Mrs. Standish. This is another pair of pages in my copy of Cooking Down East that are heavily spattered. Recipes for Golden Cake, Hot Cake, and Fudge Frosting and Broiled Coconut Icing also appear on the pages. Can we bet that it was the Blueberry Cake recipe that the owner used repeatedly?

2 eggs separated

1 cup sugar

¼ teaspoon salt

½ cup shortening

1 teaspoon vanilla

1½ cups sifted flour

1 teaspoon baking powder

⅓ cup milk

1½ cups fresh blueberries

Beat egg whites until stiff. Add about ¼ cups of the sugar to keep them stiff.

Cream shortening, add salt and vanilla to this. Add remaining sugar gradually. Add unbeaten egg yolks and beat until light and creamy. Add sifted dry ingredients alternately with milk. Fold in beaten egg whites. Fold in the fresh blueberries. (Take a bit of the flour called for in recipe and gently shake berries in it so they won't settle.)

Turn into a greased 8- by 8-inch pan. Sprinkle top of batter lightly with granulated sugar. Bake at 350 degrees for 50 to 60 minutes.

Serves 8.

BLUEBERRY GINGERBREAD

½ cup shortening

½ teaspoon salt

1 cup sugar

1 egg

2 cups flour

½ teaspoon ginger

1 teaspoon cinnamon

1 teaspoon soda

3 tablespoons molasses

1 cup sour milk or buttermilk

1 cup Maine blueberries chopped raisins may be substituted for blueberries.

3 tablespoons sugar

Cream shortening. Add salt. Add sugar gradually. Add egg then beat mixture until light and creamy. Sift and measure flour. Sift with ginger and cinnamon.

Measure soda into buttermilk or sour milk. (If you do not have either and want to "sour" milk, then use 1 cup sweet milk and add 2 tablespoons vinegar.) Stir soda to dissolve in sour milk.

Add sifted dry ingredients and sour milk alternately to creamed mixture. Add 3 tablespoons molasses.

Add blueberries. Turn batter into greased and floured 9- by 9-inch pan. Sprinkle 3 tablespoons sugar over top of batter. Bake at 350 degrees for 50 to 60 minutes.

Serves 8.

OLD FASHIONED HERMITS

1 stick margarine

¼ teaspoons alt

1 cup sugar

½ teaspoon vanilla

1 egg

½ cup milk

2¼ cups flour

½ teaspoon salt

1 teaspoon cream of tartar

¼ teaspoon cloves

¼ teaspoon allspice

¼ teaspoon cinnamon

¼ teaspoon nutmeg

1 cup chopped raisins

Cream margarine. Add vanilla and salt. Add sugar gradually. Add egg then beat until mixture is light and creamy.

Sift flour, measure, sift together with the soda, cream of tartar, and spices. Add alternately to creamed mixture with milk.

Raisins may be ground or chopped. Add and mix well, then drop this mixture by spoonfuls onto greased cookie sheets.

Bake at 400 degrees for 10 to 12 minutes.

Makes 4 to 5 dozen hermits.

DROP MOLASSES COOKIES

¼ cup shortening

½ cup boiling water

1 teaspoon salt

½ cup molasses

½ cup granulated sugar

1 egg

2½ cups flour

1 teaspoon baking powder

½ teaspoon soda

1 teaspoon ginger

1 teaspoon cinnamon

Place shortening in a bowl. Pour in boiling water. Add salt. Stir in molasses and sugar. Add egg and beat well.

Sift flour, measure and sift together with baking powder, soda, ginger, and cinnamon. Stir into mixture.

Drop by spoonfuls onto greased cookie sheet. Bake at 375 degrees for 12 to 15 minutes.

Makes 24 to 30 cookies

LIZZIES— A CHRISTMAS COOKIE

½ cup butter

1½ cups brown sugar

4 eggs

3 tablespoons milk

3 cups flour

3 teaspoon soda

1 teaspoon cinnamon

1 teaspoon nutmeg

1 pound white raisins

1 pound candies cherries

1 pound candied pineapple

1 eight-ounce package dates (optional)

4 to 6 cups pecans

½ cup orange juice

1 teaspoon vanilla

Cream butter. Add sugar slowly. Add eggs one at a time, beating after each addition. Add milk and vanilla.

Sift flour, measure, sift together with dry ingredients. Mix fruit and nuts, then flour these with one cupful of the flour mixture. Add remainder of flour mixture to creamed mixture.

Add floured fruit and nuts along with orange juice. Drop by teaspoonfuls onto greased cookie sheet. Bake in slow oven at 250 degrees for 15 to 20 minutes.

Store in tightly covered tins in cool place or freeze. Keeps like fruit cake. This recipe "halves" very well.

Makes 14 dozen cookies.

WHOOPSIE PIES

½ cup shortening

1 cup sugar

2 egg yolks beaten until light-colored

5 tablespoons cocoa

2 cups sifted flour

1 teaspoon baking powder

1 teaspoon soda

1 teaspoon salt

1 cup milk

1 teaspoon vanilla

TO MAKE FILLING

½ cup shortening

2 cups confectioner's sugar

2 egg whites

¼ teaspoon salt

1 teaspoon vanilla

This recipe came from Bangor and never was called whoopee pies, but whoopsie. That made the recipe different from the start. The filling is easy to make.

Cream shortening and sugar together, then add beaten egg yolks. Sift together cocoa, flour, baking powder, soda, and salt, then add alternately to the creamed mixture with milk and vanilla.

Drop by teaspoonfuls onto ungreased cookie sheets. Bake at 375 for 8 to 10 minutes, depending on the size of cookies you make.

Let cookies cool. Then put together with filling (see below) and wrap each separately in waxed paper.

Beat egg whites until very stiff. Fold in some of the confectioners' sugar. Cream shortening. Add remainder of sugar and add more if needed. Add salt and vanilla. Fold in the beaten whites. (Not cooked.)

BRAMBLES

Brambles, an early kind of square with a raisin filling, is a forerunner of similar bars we bake now. I hope you still bake brambles. You need not confine yourself to a raisin filling. I recall them best during my Farmington days. A classmate's mother was almost sure to include them in her returned laundry case. This is her recipe.

2 cups pie crust mix

1 cup seeded raisins (kind with the seed in)

1 cup sugar

1 egg

Grated rind and juice of 1 lemon

½ teaspoon salt

1 tablespoon cracker crumbs

Combine pastry mix with cold water and divide into two portions. Roll one portion into a large rectangular sheet and place on cookie sheet. Spread with cooled raisin mixture (see below).

Roll other pastry. Place on top of raisin mixture. Turn a bit of the edge of lower crust up over edge of upper crust, all around, and flute the edge. Take a paring knife and gently mark off the top crust into 24 squares. (Don't cut through pastry). Use a fork to prick two sets of holes in each square.

Bake at 450 degrees for 15 to 20 minutes. Remove from oven. Allow to cool a few minutes. Then cut the brambles and place on rack to cool.

BRAMBLES

TO MAKE RAISIN MIXTURE

Put raisins through food grinder, then mix with sugar, salt, beaten egg, lemon juice and rind, and cracker crumbs. Cook slowly over a low heat until thickened. Allow to cool.

BROWNIES

Mrs. Standish doesn't say "cocoa" in this recipe, but that is what she surely used. These days brownies are ubiquitous and chocolate seems to have displaced molasses in frequency of use. At the time this recipe was written down and even until fairly recently, a square of chocolate equaled 1 ounce. The product has been changed so that the squares are thinner and cooks have to be alert when making an older recipe to make sure they use enough of them to equal the 1-ounce square formerly available.

½ cup shortening

1 cup sugar

2 eggs

2 squares chocolate

⅔ cup flour

½ teaspoon salt

1 teaspoon vanilla

½ cup chopped nuts

Cream shortening, add salt, vanilla, and sugar gradually. Add eggs one at a time, beating after each addition. Add melted and cooled chocolate. Add sifted flour and chopped nuts. Turn into buttered 8 x 8-inch pan. Bake at 350 degrees for 30 minutes. Do not overcook or they will be hard.

GILLIE WHOOPERS

½ cup shortening

¾ cup sugar

2 eggs

¾ cup sifted flour

¼ teaspoon baking powder

¼ teaspoon salt

2 tablespoons cocoa

1 teaspoon vanilla

½ cup chopped nuts

TO MAKE FROSTING

½ cup light brown sugar

¼ cup water

2 squares chocolate

3 tablespoons butter

1 teaspoon vanilla

1½ cup confectioner's sugar

Mrs. Standish offers no explanation for the name of this brownie variation which appears in Maine cookbooks and even at Moody's Diner in Waldoboro. The word "Whopper" also appears sometimes as the name and the recipe always needs mini-marshmallows.

Cream shortening. Add sugar. Add eggs one at a time, beating after each addition. Add sifted dry ingredients (including cocoa). Add vanilla and chopped walnut.

Turn into buttered 9 x 9-inch pan. Bake at 350 degrees 25 minutes.

Remove from oven and sprinkle miniature marshmallows all over top, but keep away from edges of pan. Put back in oven for two minutes.

Remove from oven and frost (see below).

Boil brown sugar, water, and chocolate three minutes, then add remaining ingredients. Mix and spread over marshmallow. Allow to cool in pan and cut in squares.

"HELLO DOLLY" SQUARES

These are not State-of-Mainish in any way, except just about everyone in Maine makes them."

1 stick butter

1 cup graham crumbs

1 cup flaked coconut

1 cup semi-sweet chocolate bits

1 cup chopped nuts

1 cup sweetened condensed milk

Melt butter in 9 x 9-inch pan. Sprinkle in layers the graham crackers, coconut, unmelted chocolate bits, and nuts. (One layer each.) Pour condensed milk on top.

Bake at 350 degrees for 30 minutes. Cool in pan. Cut in very small squares.

BAKED INDIAN PUDDING

1 quart milk

¼ cup cornmeal

1 teaspoon salt

½ cup molasses

1 teaspoon cinnamon

½ teaspoon ginger

Scald 1 pint of the milk. Mix cornmeal, salt, molasses, cinnamon, and ginger. Add slowly to scalded milk. Continue stirring and cook until mixture is thickened.

Turn into well-buttered casserole dish. Bake for 1 hour at 300 degrees.

Pour remaining pint of cold milk into casserole. Stir all together. Continue Baking at 300 degrees for 2 hours.

Serve warm with thick cream, whipped cream, or vanilla ice cream.

OLD FASHIONED TARTS

When my husband was growing up and holiday time rolled around, there were sure to be old-fashioned tarts topped with a spoonful of apple jelly. His mother was famous for these and they always were made for holiday gatherings.

1 cup lard

1 egg white

1 teaspoon baking powder

1 teaspoon salt

1 tablespoon sugar

5 tablespoon cold water

About 5 cups sifted flour

Lard is the shortening mentioned and for excellent flavor and texture it cannot be surpassed. If you have a 1-pound package, then halve it, for that is just one cup. Allow lard to stand at room temperature until soft. Use a wooden spoon and beat until light and fluffy. Beat egg white until stiff. Add to beaten lard alternately with sifted dry ingredients. The 5 tablespoons of cold water may be combined at this time, too.

Roll dough to a little more than ¼ inch thick. Cut half of dough with cookie cutter, other half with doughnut cutter, (of same size). Place pastry without hole on ungreased cookie sheet and place doughnut cut rounds on top. Dip your fingers in milk and brush over the top of each tart.

Bake at 425 degrees for about 15 minutes.

OLD FASHIONED TARTS

Cool and store in air-tight container. At serving time, put spoonful of jelly in indentations.

Makes 16 tarts.

BEST NEEDHAMS

Mrs. Standish's Needhams recipe has become the standard for homemade Maine Needhams, whose naming has obscure and unverifiable origins, but which may very well have been the product of confectionary shops that migrated into home kitchens on the backs of leftover mashed potatoes.

¾ cup mashed potato

½ teaspoon salt

2 one-pound packages confectioners' sugar

1 stick margarine

½ pound flaked cocoanut

2 teaspoons vanilla

Pare and cook potato to make three-fourths cup mashed potato (not seasoned). Add salt. Using a double boiler place stick margarine in it and melt over boiling point. Add mashed potato, confectioners' sugar, flaked coconut, and vanilla.

Mix well, then turn into a buttered jelly roll pan. Spread evenly. Set in a cool place to harden. When hard, cut into small squares and dip in chocolate (see below). This recipe halves easily.

Makes 66 good-sized Needhams.

Use double boiler again. Place paraffin in top over boiling water to melt. Then add the two kinds of chocolate. Allow chocolate to melt. Stir well to mix ingredients.

BEST NEEDHAMS

TO MAKE NEEDHAMS CHOCOLATE DIP

1 twelve-ounce package chocolate bits

4 squares unsweetened chocolate

½ cake paraffin (2½ by 2½) (Yes, the same paraffin you melt to put on top of jelly)

A toothpick or cake tester may be used to dip the needham squares. Hold each square above chocolate mixture after dipping so the square drains well. Place on waxed paper to harden.

MAINE BLUEBERRY PIE

Pastry for two-crust pie

4 cups blueberries

1 cup sugar

2 tablespoons flour

Dash of salt

¼ teaspoon nutmeg

¼ teaspoon cinnamon

1 tablespoon butter

Line pie plate with pastry. Mix sugar and flour, spread about one fourth of it on lower crust. Fill with blueberries. Sprinkle remainder of sugar mix over them. Add salt, sprinkle with nutmeg and cinnamon. Dot with butter. Adjust top crust over this, then flute edges. Be sure to cut slits in crust. Bake at 425 degrees for 40 minutes. Place pie on rack to cool.

OLD FASHIONED RHUBARB PIE

Pastry for two-crust pie

4 cups unpeeled rhubarb, cut in 1-inch pieces

1½ cups sugar

6 tablespoons flour

Dash of salt

2 tablespoons butter

Line a 9-inch pie plate with pastry, leaving a half inch overhanging edge. Mix two tablespoons of flour with two tablespoons of sugar and sprinkle over the pastry. Heap the rhubarb over this mixture. Mix the remaining flour and sugar together, sprinkle over the rhubarb. Add dash of salt. Dot with butter. Adjust top crust over this, bring lower crust up over top crust and flute edges. Be sure to cut slits in crust. Bake at 450 degrees for 15 minutes, and then at 350 degrees or 45 minutes. Place pie on rack to cool.

SPUMONI CAKE

Spumoni cake is a heritage recipe from North Anson. Imagine the delight of the person who shared her family's recipe to learn that a South Portland woman used it and now, at holiday time, she makes them "by the dozen" for her church and to share with her family.

1 stick margarine

1 cup sugar

1 teaspoon vanilla

2 cups sifted flour

2 teaspoons baking powder

½ teaspoon salt

1 cup evaporated milk

Green food coloring

1 cup chopped nuts

10 diced maraschino cherries

2 tablespoons milk

1 tablespoon cocoa

Cream margarine, sugar, vanilla, and eggs, using mixer if you have one; beat on high until light and fluffy. Sift dry ingredients together three times, then turn into bowl with creamed mixture. Make two or three "wells," and turn evaporated milk into the wells. Mix on low speed just enough to blend. Divide batter into three parts.

Add 4 drops green color and chopped nuts to one batter.

Add diced maraschino cherries and a few drops cherry juice to the second batter.

Blend milk with cocoa and add to third batter.

Grease and flour a 9x5x3-inch loaf pan, spoon batter into prepared pan in 1, 2, 3 order.

Bake 1 hour at 325 degrees. Cool, wrap, and

store in a cool place and allow to ripen.

This cake is placed on a board and sliced thin, to show off its marbled effect. Spumoni cake is reminiscent of what our mothers used to make and yet it is as up-to-dates as many cake we might choose.

DAFFODIL CAKE

Probably this cake recipe has been in my files as long as any, and I am certain I have made more of them than any other cake of this type. A combination of sponge cake and angel cake in marbled effect will conjure up thoughts of the past, and you will find it a welcome treat now.

This is a good cake for birthdays. If yours is a fat-free diet, this is an answer, too. The first year I worked for the power company as a home service advisor, I was given the recipe by a woman in Fryeburg. She told me it was Mrs. Pike's cake recipe. I never met her, but I have liked using her recipe.

6 eggs separated

1¼ cups sugar

1 cup sifted cake flour

½ teaspoon cream of tartar

½ teaspoon vanilla

¼ teaspoon almond extract

½ teaspoon lemon extract

White batter: Beat 6 egg whites until foamy. Add ¼ teaspoon of the salt, the almond flavoring, and vanilla. Sprinkle cream of tartar over the foamy whites. Continue to beat until they hold up in peaks. Fold in ¾ cup of the sugar. Fold in ½ cup of the sifted flour. Set bowl aside.

Yellow batter: Beat 6 egg yolks until light colored and thick. Add 2 tablespoons cold water and lemon extract. Beat well. Beat in remaining ½ cup sugar. Sift remaining ½

DAFFODIL CAKE

½ teaspoon baking powder

½ teaspoon salt

2 tablespoons cold water

cup cake flour together with remaining ¼ teaspoon salt and the ½ teaspoon baking powder, then fold into beaten egg yolks.

Use large angel cake tin. Do not grease it. Alternate white and yellow batter so you have a marbled effect.

Bake at 325 degrees for 60 to 70 minutes. Invert pan and allow cake to cool 1 hour before removing it.

LOVELIGHT CHOCOLATE CAKE

Everyone has a favorite chocolate cake recipe. This one happens to be mine. I've been scolded several times because it did not appear in *Cooking Down East*. It is a comfortable feeling to know I have a second chance.

2 eggs, separated

1½ cups sugar

2 squares chocolate, melted

1⅔ cups sifted flour

¾ teaspoon soda

¾ teaspoon salt

⅓ cup cooking oil

1 cup buttermilk

1 teaspoon vanilla

Melt chocolate, allow to cool slightly before adding to batter. Beat the egg whites until they hold up in shape, then add ½ cup of the sugar to beaten whites and set aside.

Sift flour, measure and sift together with remaining sugar, soda, and salt into a large bowl. Add oil and ½ cup of the buttermilk to the dry ingredients. Use mixer and beat at low speed for1 minute. Add remaining buttermilk, the unbeaten egg yolks, the cooled chocolate, and the vanilla. Beat 1 minute at medium speed. Fold in the beaten egg whites and sugar mixture. Turn batter into a greased and lightly floured 9 x 9-inch pan.

Bake 1 hour at 350 degrees. Place pan on rack to cool for about 5 minutes, then turn cake onto rack to complete cooling.

LOVELIGHT CHOCOLATE CAKE

WHITE MOUNTAIN ICING FOR LOVELIGHT CHOCOLATE CAKE

1 cup sugar

⅓ cup water

Pinch of salt

1 egg white, stiffly beaten

½ teaspoon vanilla

Beat egg white stiffly and add salt. Cook sugar and water together in a saucepan, stirring until sugar dissolves. Then cook without stirring, using a medium heat, until syrup forms a thread when dropped from the tip of a spoon.

Remove from heat and pour in a thin steam over beaten egg white. Add vanilla and continue beating with electric mixer until it reaches the right consistency to spread. Frost only the top of cake. If you wish, melt 1 square cooking chocolate, add about ½ teaspoon margarine to make it appear glossy, and dribble this melted mixture all over top of frosting. Do this just before frosting 'sets.' Allow to harden before cutting

HEATH BAR SQUARES

For more years than I can recall, she has been signing her letters, 'Sal.' She lives in Rockland. It was Sal who compelled me to always write "Happy Cooking" when I autographed *Cooking Down East*, for that is the way she has always signed her letters. One day she signed, "Keep Cooking," and so named my second cookbook, *Keep Cooking the Maine Way*. This is a favorite recipe of Sal's

1 stick margarine

1 cup brown sugar

½ cup white sugar

2 cups sifted flour

¼ teaspoon salt

1 egg beaten

1 cup buttermilk

1 teaspoon soda

1 teaspoon vanilla

6 Heath Bars crushed

Combine margarine, sugars, flour, and salt in a bowl, using a pastry blender and cutting in margarine as for pie crust. Remove ½ cup of mixture to be used for topping.

Beat egg and add to remaining mixture. Combine soda with buttermilk, add to mixture. Add vanilla and mix thoroughly. Turn into buttered 9- x 13-inch pan. Top with reserved mixture.

Placing Heath Bars on wax paper on a cutting board, cover with foil and, with a hammer, lightly tap and crush bars. Sprinkle all over top of batter.

Bake at 350 degrees for 30 minutes. Place pan on rack to cool, cut in squares.

OLD FASHIONED CHOCOLATE FUDGE

2 cups sugar

$^{2}/_{3}$ cup milk

2 squares chocolate

2 tablespoons light corn syrup

2 tablespoons butter

1 teaspoon vanilla

1 cup coarsely chopped walnuts

Cut up chocolate and put with sugar, milk, and corn syrup into saucepan and cook slowly, stirring until sugar is dissolved and boiling point is reached. Reduce heat and cook without stirring, but don't let it burn, until 236 degrees is reached on a candy thermometer or, when tested in cold water, it forms a soft ball.

Add butter and vanilla, but do not stir while cooling. When lukewarm, beat until fudge has lost its shiny look and when a small amount dropped from a spoon will hold its shape. Add chopped walnut, pour into greased pan. When cold, cut into squares.

MONROE SQUASH PIE

Pastry for one-crust pie

1½ cups cooked squash, strained, or use canned squash

¼ cup sugar

½ teaspoon salt

¼ teaspoon cinnamon

¼ teaspoon ginger

¼ teaspoon nutmeg

2 eggs, beaten lightly

1¾ cups light cream, scalded (The Monroe admonition was, "if you don't have the cream, don't make the pie.")

This squash pie has always been a mystery to me—mostly because it is from a faded old column in a newspaper . . . . it is a wonderful recipe for squash pie . . . . used by the writer's mother. She was one of six sisters, but the mystery is that I cannot tell if it is a recipe from Monroe, Maine, or if the family name was Monroe. I always felt a man wrote that column, for he stated, "Squash is a 'keeping' vegetable, for use all through the months while God is writing with the chalk of winter on the blackboard of the land."

Canned squash will be the easy way to make this pie. It is what I use. Mix squash with sugar, salt, and spices. Add lightly beaten eggs. Stir in the scalded cream.

MONROE SQUASH PIE

Fit pastry onto a 9-inch pie plate, flute edge. Pour filling into unbaked pastry. Bake 15 minutes at 450 degrees, lower heat to 325 degrees and bake 35 minutes longer.

CHOCOLATE CREAM PIE

That wonderful old standard, chocolate cream pie, is a favorite. This recipe came from Prospect Harbor—now that is really down east. This woman's daughter, who lives in Gardiner, says she had never found a chocolate pie as good as her mother used to make. I will vouch for that and you will, too, if you have ever sampled it at one of the card parties held for the benefit of the Gardiner General Hospital.

1½ cups milk, scalded in top of double boiler

2 egg yolks

1 cup sugar

3 tablespoons flour

3 tablespoons cocoa

¼ teaspoon salt

1 teaspoon vanilla

1 tablespoon butter

2 egg whites, saved for meringue topping.

This recipe is for an 8-inch baked pie shell. If you have a 10-inch pie in mind, double the amount of the filling with the thought you will have extra, which you can use for pudding.

Reserve 4 tablespoons of the sugar for making the meringue. In making meringue, it is 2 tablespoons sugar to 1 egg white.

Mix remaining sugar, flour, cocoa, and salt; beat 2 egg yolks and combine with dry mixture. Add small amount of scalded milk to mixture, stir, then pour back into top of double boiler. Stir constantly over boiling water until thickened. Cover and cook about 6 minutes longer. Stir in butter.

CHOCOLATE CREAM PIE

Remove from heat, allow to cool. Add vanilla. Turn into baked pie shell. Top with meringue, bake as directed for meringue.

Many people prefer whipped topping on chocolate cream pie. If so, use all the sugar in this filling. But do not add egg whites, for the filling would be too runny.

JUDGE PETERS PUDDING

If ever a recipe has stood the test of time it has to be Judge Peters Pudding. In 1883 John A. Peters of Bangor was appointed Chief Justice of the Maine Supreme Court. This was his favorite dessert, which he enjoyed especially at holiday time. It is not at all the sort of recipe you might expect at the turn of the century, and we like to think he will be remembered among other things for this fine dessert.

2 envelopes plain gelatin in, each envelope is 1 tablespoon

½ cup fresh orange juice

1 cup sugar

2 oranges cut in pieces

2 bananas sliced

6 figs, cut small

9 dates, cut small

10 walnuts coarsely broken

Juice of 2 lemons

Soak 2 envelopes plain gelatin in ½ cup cold water. Add 1 cup boiling water. Add orange juice and sugar. Stir to dissolve ingredients and chill until syrupy.

Combine fruit (when preparing fruits, use kitchen shears dipped in hot water. It makes the job go faster), walnuts, and lemon juice in a bowl. Once the gelatin mixture has begun to congeal, fold in the fruit mixture, blend well.

Pour into a mold and chill until set. Custard cups make good molds for individual servings. Top with whipped cream or a custard sauce, although it is also delicious just as it is.

BLUEBERRY FLUMMERY

This recipe stirs memories. The summer I cooked at Camp Brookline, a girls' camp in Bridgton, this was their favorite dessert. It could have been because the girls picked their own blueberries. We called it blueberry bread and butter pudding. Come to find out, it is named Blueberry Flummery. The recipe is as old as New England. It is simple to make and delicious.

8 slices bread, buttered

1 quart blueberries

1 cup sugar

1 teaspoon salt

Whipped topping

Wash the berries, place in saucepan, add sugar and salt, cook over low heat to summering point. Cook for 10 minutes.

Butter bread generously. Trim crusts. Alternate layers of buttered bread and hot stewed blueberries until all are used, ending with fruit and juice. Bake at 350 degrees for 20 minutes.

Chill in refrigerator. Top with whipped cream flavored with nutmeg.

Marjorie Standish made a point of using recipes she knew had been handed down mother to daughter over generations of Maine cooks and she stoutly defended cooking from scratch. Still, here and there in her recipes, you can see the hard work of her fellow home economists laboring in test kitchens: the frequent use of canned soups, for instance, as sauces for casseroles. Her salads often called for quite a lot of packaged gelatin (that is, Jello). Modern ingredients like canned pineapple, pimentos, and processed cheese joined canned tomatoes, mushrooms, clams, corn, and others that were a far cry from rural seasonal Maine farmhouse fare.

In *Cooking Down East* hardly any of her cakes or desserts called for prepared mixes or commercial ingredients except for marshmallows, condensed milk, and chocolate chips. In *Keep Cooking the Maine Way*, however, Mrs. Standish prefaced the baking chapter by writing, "Packaged mixes, convenience foods, and the cooking short cuts available in our markets are appealing, but cooks know they can become costly. Also there is the matter of pride. Maine cooks like to keep alive the tradition of 'cooking from scratch' and they hand down family recipes to provide enchanted eating."

But things were changing, Mrs. Standish acknowledged, as she noted, "This chapter on desserts includes many of these [from scratch recipes], as well as those on the Now side." Sure enough, a few recipes appeared consisting of package cake mixes doctored up with pudding mixes, extra oil, or more eggs.

Luckily for us, enough of Mrs. Standish's from scratch-recipes are perfectly replicable so we can continue to enjoy her cookery. Any, however, that rely on products like marshmallows are at risk of failing because those products have been reformulated over the past 75 to 80 years and simply don't combine with other ingredients as they used to. Cake and pudding mixes may or may not work together as they did earlier. It is safer for cooks to look for the most recent recipe they can find for some of those dishes.

Can sizes have changed, too; in some cases, the two- or three-ounce difference in can size from fifty years ago to today can be easily compensated for by adding a little more from a second can or amplifying with water or broth. Often, Mrs. Standish provides a cup measurement of a canned ingredient like tomatoes or broth so can size is irrelevant.

Even though our flour may be different from the flour of 200 hundred years ago, we can still make a fairly close replication of a historical recipe. This recent phenomenon, however, of disappearing ingredients, like those marshmallows replaced with reformulated versions, means that there may be hundreds of essentially extinct recipes in the future, an odd thing to ponder.

10 Game Cookery

In Maine, many of the methods we use for cooking game have been passed along by word of mouth from one generation to another and from one Maine family to another. These are family recipes for the most part. With a father who hunted and a husband who hunts, the recipes that follow are the result of cooking a lot of well-cared for game.

ROAST WILD DUCK

"Maine provides one of the most noted duck-hunting areas in the East at the mouth of the Kennebec River—Merrymeeting Bay," wrote Mrs. Standish. This recipe was her mother's preferred recipe.

Clean and dress the duck. Salt the inside. Stuff with quartered raw onion and cored, quartered raw apple. These will be discarded after roasting. Salt and pepper outside of bird, lay 2 or 3 slices salt pork or bacon on breasts, secure with toothpicks. Place in covered roaster or cover with foil in shallow pan. Roast at 350 for 2 hours.

And then there are gourmet cooks who will have none of this old-fashioned Maine nonsense regarding roasting wild ducks. They like seeing the trickle of blood that follows the point of the carving knife as the duck is served. Just in case you like yours rare, use the raw onion and apple quarters, roast at 400 degrees 15 minutes, then reduce heat to 350 allowing 15 minutes per pound in all.

TO FRY VENISON

Use your heavy black fry pan. Heat pan very hot. Lay steak or chops in pan on high heat. Sear meat on both sides, lower heat and cook to degree of doneness your family likes. If no marinade is used, salt and pepper steak or chops as they cook.

This is the way many Maine cooks fry venison, using no fat at all and the high heat for searing the meat, then lowering the heat for two or three minutes on a side to complete the cooking.

I favor a medium heat all through the cooking, using a small amount of margarine or butter in the fry pan. Cooking the meat more gently, allowing four or five minutes on a side.

If you decide upon a marinade, make it a simple one, using only one-third as much vinegar as oil, salt and pepper, in other words a French dressing. Allow the venison to soak in the marinade for several hours. This can apply to steaks, chops, and roasts.

VENISON MINCEMEAT

Maine housewives set great store by mincemeat made with venison. This recipe was used many years in a Gardiner household. It has appeared in my column and is now used all over Maine.

Mincemeat, a centuries-old way of preserving meat for winter use, is the best use of venison neck meat. A long deer neck, bony and covered with tough, stringy meat needs cooking and chopping to make it useful. Mrs. Standish's recipe is notable for its use of molasses to sweeten it in addition to brown sugar. The recipe predates our familiar seedless raisins; in past times raisins, which are dried grapes, still contained seeds that had to be removed, leaving a large raisin, hence the instructions to "cut in pieces." This recipe also reflects the Temperance leanings of the Gardiner family who, like many Mainers of the 19th century, eschewed alcohol. Traditional mincemeat recipes contained hard cider or brandy.

About 5 pounds venison neck meat

2 pounds suet

Cover meat and suet with boiling water and cook until tender. Cool in water in which they are cooked. Suet will rise to top, forming cake of fat, which may be easily removed. Cook

VENISON MINCEMEAT

20 cups chopped apples (parings may be left on or not)

4 pounds brown sugar

3 cups molasses

4 quarts apple cider

4 pounds seeded raisins, cut in pieces

3 pounds currants

½ pound citron, finely chopped

¼ pound each candied orange peel, lemon, grapefruit peel, candied cherries

1 quart grape juice

1½ tablespoons nutmeg

1½ tablespoons cinnamon

1 tablespoon powdered cloves

Salt to taste

this stock down by boiling so there is 1½ cups. Chop venison, you should have about ten cups of cooked ground meat. Chop the suet.

Pare, quarter, and core apples. Chop them, combine with chopped cooked venison and suet. Add sugar, molasses, cider, raisins, currants, citron, candied fruit peels. Add boiled-down stock. Mix well.

Cook slowly 2 hours, then add grape juice and spices. Mix very carefully making sure mixture is hot, turn into hot, sterilized jars. Seal.

Makes 29 pints.

11 | Preserving

Habit is strong. Part of the process of getting ready for winter in days gone by was the preservation of food and this is no by-gone achievement. The Maine housewife considers this part of her heritage. She has a large sized kettle, a long handled wooden spoon, jelly tumblers, jars for pickles, one big old crock for old-fashioned sour pickles. She intends to use them.

STRAWBERRY PRESERVE

Fresh strawberry preserve comes first, for it was the first recipe of this sort I ever used in "Cooking Down East."

3 pints strawberries

3 pints sugar

Put one pint sugar and one cup water into a good sized saucepan. Bring to a boil and allow to boil 15 minutes.

Add one pint strawberries and let this boil 15 minutes. Add one pint sugar and one pint strawberries. Boil all together 15 minutes.

Add another pint of strawberries and one pint of sugar and boil for another 15 minutes.

Pour into canning jars and seal.

STRAWBERRY AND RHUBARB JAM

Rhubarb combined with fruit gelatin to make jam or marmalade is very popular. The ease with which it is made, plus delicious flavor has a lot to do with this.

- 5 cups rhubarb, cut in 1-inch pieces
- 1 cup drained, crushed pineapple
- 1 three-ounce package strawberry gelatin
- 4 cups sugar

Mix rhubarb, sugar, and drained pineapple together in a large kettle and allow to stand for 30 minutes. Bring slowly to a boil and cook 12 minutes, stirring constantly. Remove from heat and add one package dry strawberry gelatin. Stir until dissolved. Pour into glasses and top with hot paraffin.

SPICED CRAB APPLES

2 pounds crab apples

4 cups sugar

1 pint vinegar

4 sticks cinnamon

Whole cloves

Wash and drain the apples, leaving on the stems. Mix sugar, vinegar, and cinnamon in a sauce pan and cook 5 minutes.

Stick a whole clove into blossom end of several of the apples, then place them into syrup and cook for 10 minutes. Put apples in pint jars (make sure two or three apples with cloves get into each jar.) Pour hot syrup in jars. Seal.

OLD FASHIONED CUCUMBER PICKLES

1 gallon water

1 cup salt

1 cup sugar

1 cup dry mustard

Combine dry ingredients. Add vinegar. Use pint or quart jars that have been washed, scalded, and wiped dry. If you are using jar rubbers, do the same with them.

Use finger length cucumbers, wash in cold water, wipe dry, pack into jars, fill with vinegar mixture (some cooks dilute the vinegar with cold water by half.) Seal.

Pickles will be ready to eat in about 2 weeks, and will keep all winter.

MUSTARD PICKLES

4 pounds slender cucumbers or enough sliced, to make 3 quarts

6 sweet red peppers

2 quarts button onions

1 large cauliflower

1 bunch celery

If available, a few tiny cucumbers

TO MAKE THE SAUCE

1 quart cider vinegar

3 tablespoons dry mustard

1½ teaspoon turmeric

1 pint cold water

1⅓ cup flour

5 cups granulated sugar

Prepare cucumbers, peppers, onions, and cauliflower; soak overnight in cold water with 1 cup salt sprinkled over these.

In morning, bring to a boil. Drain off liquid. Slice celery and add raw, sliced celery to vegetables. Add the heated sauce (see below), bring very slowly to the boiling point, and put in hot sterilized jars. Seal.

Mix all ingredients in a saucepan and heat to the boiling point.

CHILI SAUCE

- 6 pounds peeled ripe tomatoes
- 6 peeled onions
- 2 hot red peppers
- 4 seeded sweet green peppers
- 2 cups granulated sugar
- 2 tablespoon salt
- 4 cups vinegar
- 4 teaspoons whole cloves
- 4 teaspoons whole allspice
- 4 three-inch sticks cinnamon

"Maine's favorite way of using ripe tomatoes is making chili sauce," wrote Mrs. Standish in headnotes for the chili sauce recipe. This is a surprise for spaghetti and tomato sauce loving Mainers of the present. The only tomato sauce recipe in her cookbooks, appears in Cooking Down East as a sauce for Halibut! Chili sauce is delicious, and Mrs. Standish reported, "We serve it with so many Maine foods like baked beans, cod fish cakes, scrambled eggs and roast beef hash, just to mention a few."

Chop tomatoes, onions, and peppers very fine then add sugar, salt, vinegar. Add spices tied loosely in a cheesecloth bag. Cook slowly, uncovered for 2 hours or until thick. Remove spice bag. Pour into hot sterilized jars and seal immediately.

REFRIGERATED CUCUMBER PICKLES

"This delightful pickle recipe" came to Mrs. Standish when "Em" came to visit Maine friends and met her. "When Em returned to her own big farm in Nebraska, she sent this pickle recipe," which Mrs. Standish said, "pleased all Maine people. It is an uncooked pickle and is really kept refrigerated."

25 not too large cucumbers

3 onions, medium sized

½ cup pickling salt

4 cups cider vinegar

5 cups sugar

1 teaspoon turmeric

1½ teaspoons celery salt

1½ teaspoons mustard seed

Wash and wipe cucumbers. Peel onions. Slice unpared cucumbers and peeled onions for table use, making the slices thin. Mix all other ingredients and pour over slices. Mix together lightly. Place in glass jars for storage, cover jars and keep refrigerated. Delicious!

INDIAN RELISH

1 peck green tomatoes

1 cup salt

1 medium cabbage, chopped fine

3 quarts vinegar

6 onions chopped

3 hot red peppers, chopped

2 sweet green peppers, chopped

8 cups sugar

2 tablespoons celery seed

2 tablespoons mustard seed

1 tablespoon stick cinnamon

1 tablespoon whole cloves

Maybe you call it piccalilli but my mother always called it Indian Pickle. There was always a crock of it down cellar at the farm and we liked it best with baked beans.

Chop green tomatoes, sprinkle with salt. Let set overnight. Drain. Then add cabbage and vinegar.

Boil slowly for 30 minutes. Then add onions, peppers, sugar, celery seed, and mustard seed.

Mix this together. Then make a small cheese cloth bag, put cinnamon and whole cloves into bag and tie securely, then place in pickle mixture.

Cook all together until vegetables are soft. Ladle into sterilized jars and seal immediately.

12 | Firsts Are Last (Appetizers)

So it has become quite natural during this interlude before everybody assembles, to serve appetizers or a tray of snacks with drinks of the guest's choice. The Happy Hour we call it, and a pleasant interlude it is.

These [recipes] fit into a Maine cookbook only because, without exception, all the recipes have been sent to me by Maine people. These really are "firsts," for they were the first recipes for dips I used in my column.

MINCED CLAM DIP

1 can minced clams

1 eight-ounce package cream cheese

Allow cream cheese to soften to room temperature. Drain canned clams. Mash cheese, add 2 tablespoons cream, if necessary. Add drained clams, salt, and pepper to taste. Serve with crackers or potato chips.

HOT CRABMEAT DIP

1 eight-ounce package cream cheese

1 can crabmeat

1 dash Worcestershire sauce (sherry may be added)

A little lemon juice

Sliced almonds for the top if you wish

Mix all together and put into a small casserole. Bake at 350 degrees until cream cheese is "gooey," about 20 to 25 minutes. Keep hot to serve with crackers.

SNAPPY COCKTAIL SAUCE

½ cup chili sauce

½ cup tomato catsup

⅓ cup lemon juice

3 tablespoons horse-radish

½ teaspoon salt

½ teaspoon onion salt

2 teaspoons Worcestershire sauce

4 drops Tabasco sauce

Mix all ingredients thoroughly.

SUNBEAMS

You may call these delicious cheese cookies "sunbeams," it is one name for them. This recipe came from Gardiner, where it is widely used. You will find them popular at any kind of party.

¼ pound butter

½ pound sharp cheddar cheese

1 cup sifted flour

¼ teaspoon salt

Dash of cayenne pepper

Cream butter, using a large spoon. Add cheddar cheese by grating on a coarse grater so that the mixture will be smooth. Add flour slowly. Add seasonings and mix well.

Make into 3 rolls, as in making refrigerator cookies. Wrap in wax paper or foil, if you wish to freeze them for later baking. Store in refrigerator or freeze. Remove when ready to bake. Slice in thin slices, place on greased cookie sheet. Bake at 425 degrees for 5 to 6 minutes.

PERCOLATOR PUNCH [A PERIOD PIECE]

1 tablespoon whole cloves

1½ teaspoon whole allspice

3 two-inch pieces broken cinnamon sticks

¼ teaspoon salt

½ cup light brown sugar

3 cups water

3 cups pineapple juice

Place pineapple juice and water in a 9-cup percolator. Place remaining ingredients in the percolator basket. Perk for 10 minutes. Remove the basket and serve hot.

Serves 8 to 10.